The Small Town
Big Kitchen Cookbook

Helen,
Enjoy!
Best Wishes
Annette   5/15/04

The Small Town Big Kitchen Cookbook

Cooking with Family and Friends

Annette Marie Vitalone

Foreword by Anthony Michael Vitalone

iUniverse, Inc.
New York Lincoln Shanghai

The Small Town Big Kitchen Cookbook
Cooking with Family and Friends

iUniverse, Inc.

For information address:
iUniverse
2021 Pine Lake Road, Suite 100
Lincoln, NE 68512
www.iuniverse.com

ISBN: 0-595-29161-9

Printed in the United States of America

To my son Anthony, you have been my mentor, confidant, and friend. Your inspiration made this cookbook a reality.

And

In loving memory of my mom, who taught me the gift of giving and sharing.

"I don't measure."

—Antoinette Theresa Muscato (Mom)

CONTENTS

FOREWORD

The first memory I have of my mom is the two of us sitting on the sofa eating my favorite lunch on TV trays after my first day at pre-school. I can still taste the baked clam strips and tomato soup with oyster crackers. I do not remember the days leading up to pre-school, getting dressed that morning or even what I did that first day. However, I remember the special lunch my mom made for me. People express their love for others in many ways. Some give expensive gifts, others are good providers and a few very special people show their love for others in the food they cook. For these select few, like my mom, cooking is more than an obligation to one's family or even a hobby; it is truly a labor of love.

I remember when I was growing up; it was pretty impressive for someone to have multiple television sets, a home computer or even an Atari video game. Bragging rights for my siblings and me were more in the lines of having two full-sized freezers in our basement! Although not a rallying point for after school activities; in retrospect, I would not have traded them for any video game. You see, they were always filled with a bounty of homemade foods: zucchini bread, pumpkin bread, banana bread, diced squash, corn on the cob, rhubarb, strawberry jam, grape jam, apricot jam, raspberry jam, apple pies, peach pies, cherry pies, and my favorite strawberry-rhubarb pies and the list goes on. My dad's labors during the summer in the garden were rewarded all year long in mom's cooking—truly a divine partnership. For the most part, just one freezer was in use during the year, however, around Thanksgiving, mom would crank up the second freezer and begin to fill it—and I mean fill it—with a variety of homemade Italian Christmas cookies. I would get so excited when mom would sit down and say to everyone 'OK, what cookies do you want this year?' It was by far the best Christmas List to write. Mom would keep that list on the side of the refrigerator and mark them off with the number of cookies she had made—pretty much like Santa would with his List. For a number of years, the count of cookies well surpassed 2,000 and she still has all her lists to prove it. Needless to say, that freezer was locked and the key 'hidden', however, one of dad's hand made screwdrivers did the job just fine if mom's new hiding place was not yet found. To this day mom still prepares loads of cookies and the time and effort she puts into her Christmas cookies is truly a labor of love. Mom has said to me time and time again, that she receives so much enjoyment from bringing a dish or tray of cookies to her family and friends as a gift. If you have been fortunate enough to receive such a gift, you understand just how special this gift is. From personal experience, to receive a care package of home made Italian Christmas cookies during final exams while at college was better than any gift I would receive on Christmas morning—truly a gift from the heart.

Growing up was one social gathering after another where food, family and friends all came together. We lived in a beautiful two-story home with an entry foyer, a formal dining room and an additional formal living room that had a 20 foot vaulted ceiling. It was a beautiful home to live in and an impressive space to throw parties—and throw parties is just what my mom did best. The entire year was filled with gathering of family and friends for choir groups, office holiday parties, minstrel show performers, the 'aunts and uncles', progressive dinners, birthdays, all the holidays, and special events. However, all it took was for an unexpected guest to pull in the driveway and mom would have a pie out of the freezer and into the oven before the doorbell stopped ringing. There was always a welcoming smell coming from the kitchen.

As special as the holidays were when it came to the food mom would prepare, it was even more special on birthdays. About a week prior to a household birthday, mom would ask that person celebrating the day, what they wanted for their special dinner and what type of cake they wanted. Whether it was simply homemade pizza or a request for a full Thanksgiving dinner, mom would prepare just what was requested. The dessert requests were at bit unique at times. My brother Pat and my sister Joanne would typically stick to the tradition cake, however, my Dad and I would always push for a Birthday Pie and once my brother Vinnie requested oatmeal cookies. Giving menu control to children and my dad was a risk, but mom always made it work and prepared a meal that was a gift from the heart.

I am thrilled that my mom has taken the time to share these recipes with both family and friends. The recipes included in this book have such strong memories for my family and me—it is truly a legacy of love that will be cherished.

—Anthony Michael Vitalone
Author of: The Big City Small Kitchen Cookbook:
Cooking without Time and Space

PREFACE

Someone once told me that one of life's most precious gifts is the gift of memory. When I started to reflect on my association with food, it brought back many memories of grandparents, parents, being a wife and mother, but especially memories of family and friends.

Some of my first and lasting memories involve some type of celebration, where family and friends would come together. Whether a baptism, first communion, birthday, or a wedding, there was always some type of celebration taking place, especially when you grow up in an Italian family. However, the big holidays (Thanksgiving, Easter and Christmas) have always held a special place in my heart when it comes to cooking.

I still have vivid food memories of Christmas Eve. Having the family gathered together to celebrate and enjoy a home cooked meal was what the holiday was all about to me. My mother would make traditional Italian cookies and I will never forget the images of my grandmother's pasta with chicken legs sticking out of it. To this day I still remember what my grandmother gave to my brother Frank and me each year; simply one of her large cotton stockings, filled with oranges, nuts, and apples. And somewhere hidden inside, usually at the toe, was a dollar bill. Although modest by today's standards, it was a gift of food from the heart. I expect these memories were the seeds that grew into my association of food 'giving' and preparing a feast for the holidays. Although I have never given my grandchildren a similar gift, tradition finds its way to my home where you will always find oranges, nuts and apples in a large bowl on the table during the holidays.

Thinking back to one Thanksgiving in particular, my brother Frank and I talked my dad into buying a live turkey. We wanted an old fashion Thanksgiving where you chopped the head off a live turkey; it sounded very simple to my brother and me. Well, on Thanksgiving morning, my dad took the turkey out for its final walk to an old tree stump. He carefully held the turkey down with his foot and with meticulous aim he struck the turkey and removed its head. My brother and

I were so excited, that we began to yell and run around. However, the yelling soon turned into screams of terror as our future dinner guest joined my brother and me in our running. My dad had not tied the turkey down, so that turkey took off and began to run around the backyard, with no head. Needless to say, there was a bit of laughter at the dinner table that Thanksgiving.

When I think back on my early days as a wife and mother, preparing food was a challenge. With a limited income I had to be creative. Well, my family did not always enjoy my creative cooking. There are only so many ways you can cook cubed steak. I sure could have used the television cooking channels back then. If my family had their way this would be one cut of meat that should have been outlawed in every grocery store. This was not a tender cut of meat, but your jaw sure got a good workout with all that chewing and it did keep the dinner table chatter to a minimum. To this day my children cringe if I mention the good old days when we had cubed steak for dinner. There was, however, one steak dish I prepared that my family actually enjoyed. That was my mom's Swiss steak. To prepare the steak I would dust it with seasoned flour, and then use a tenderizing wheel to work in the flour. My sons, Tony and Pat, had an ongoing battle as to who was going to inherit the wheel. I purchased this utensil over 40 years ago while living in Germany and had no idea I was acquiring a family heirloom. I would visit every gadget store each time I went to the mall to find more tenderizing wheels, but no luck. Thank goodness for modern technology as my son Pat found not only one but two tenderizer wheels on an Internet auction site. Without hesitation he purchased both, one for him and one for his sister Joanne. No more bickering and Tony has his big inheritance; 'THE WHEEL'.

There must be a gardening gene that exists in the Italian men in my family. As a child, my dad and his father Francesco, planted an amazing garden every summer. There were enough tomatoes for canning, lettuce for salads and always-extra vegetables to share with family and friends. Because of the abundance of vegetables that were grown, my grandfather would sell produce at his own vegetable stand. We all enjoyed the availability of fresh fruits and vegetables, and my brother Frank really enjoyed eating watermelon. However, one summer, at the age of about seven or eight, he just could not get enough watermelon and my dad was tired of listening to him beg for it. So, my dad decided, if you want watermelon, then you got watermelon. My dad sat him down placed a whole watermelon in front of him and said "Start eating." I cannot remember how much he ate, but I can still hear him saying he had enough. This was music to my dad's ears, but Frank still loves watermelon to this day. As an adult, my father-in-law Rocco and my husband Tony, both cultivated gardens. The tradition of always having fresh vegetables and fruit on the table continues. We still have a garden every year and I guess the tradition has been passed to the next generation, because my daughter and my sons all have a green thumb for gardening.

Reflecting upon my memories of food would not be complete without mentioning my mom, Antoinette. My mom, who was all of 4 foot 11, was an excellent cook. She was born in Quebec Canada, married my dad and came to our hometown of Canandaigua, NY in 1937. This wonderful woman was not only a devoted wife and caring mother, but she was also my best friend. On many occasions, when I would ask her for a particular recipe, her reply would simply be "I don't measure." I would stand and watch when she would make piecrust; it was a hand full of flour and a scoop of shortening, sprinkled with cold water. It was the best piecrust you would have ever tasted. So, needless to say when it came to cooking traditional family recipes, it was sink or swim on my part. Not until I sat down to write this book, did I realize just how much I followed in my mother's footsteps. There are many recipes in this cookbook that I had to prepare step by step with a measuring cup and measuring spoons by my side for the first time. I realize now that "I don't measure" either. Thank you mom for the memories.

I hope the recipes in this book create wonderful memories for you, as they have for me and my family and friends.

ACKNOWLEDGEMENT

To my Family and Friends, thank you for sharing your recipes for the past forty-five years. I have taken pride in preparing these great dishes for all of you and now the opportunity to share the recipes.

To my husband Tony, you always compliment my cooking, even if the recipe was a failure. Thank you for your support and encouraging me to write this cookbook.

INTRODUCTION

A year ago, if someone had told me that I would be publishing a cookbook, I would have laughed. After all, most people do not just wake up one morning and decide that day to undertake such a task. Then again, in my case, this was true. Last year, as a Christmas present to the entire family, my son Anthony published The Big City Small Kitchen Cookbook, which contained over 100 original recipes he had been developing for over 10 years. It was quite a surprise and proud moment for the entire family when I—unknowingly—opened the first copy and realized Anthony had published the cookbook he had been talking about most of his life. Once the excitement of the moment began to subside, Anthony presented me with a final gift. He prefaced the package with a comment that the gift was more of a 'suggestion' and it was my decision whether to accept the challenge. It turns out that the box contained an Author's Workbook from Anthony's publisher, complete with publishing guidelines, contracts, copyright agreements and even an example cover design for my own cookbook. My son had made arrangements for me to write the follow-up to his cookbook, thus the birth of The Small Town Big Kitchen Cookbook. The shock took awhile to wear off, but later that evening I sat down with Anthony and my husband Tony and decided to seize the opportunity presented to me. The past year has been a wonderful journey for me, as I have reflected on a lifetime of memories, which were in a place I never would have imagined—my recipe box. At times the journey was both happy and sad, but in the end, I realized that with each recipe a page was added to my memories of family and friends.

Unlike my son's cookbook, where the recipes are designed to be prepared in an efficiency kitchen to serve 2-4 people, this book is written to celebrate the coming together of family and friends. These are Small Town comfort foods that are meant to be prepared in a Big Kitchen and shared with many family and friends. For the most part, this is the book you want to reach for when planning a summer picnic, a holiday celebration or a comforting meal on a cold winter's night.

I am a baker at heart and therefore, a large portion of this book is dedicated to all the traditional Italian cookies, pies and pastries that have been in my family for generations. My son refers to me as a Master Baker and after all these years, perhaps I am. Baking is an exact science. Unlike cooking, when you bake, following the recipe is essential to ensure the proper results. If I can make one suggestion—based on years of experience—the trick to being a good baker is to keep your family out of the kitchen when you are measuring!

Author's Note

The author has used abbreviations for measurements in her recipes. The abbreviation for tablespoon will be shown as tblp.

APPETIZERS

BROCCOLI PUFFS

When I worked for an insurance company, this is a dish that one of my co-workers brought in for a potluck lunch

Ingredients:
20 oz. bag frozen cut up broccoli
1 can cream mushroom soup
4 oz. Shredded cheddar cheese
¼ cup milk
½ cup mayonnaise
1 beaten egg

Combine in small bowl:
¼ cup plain breadcrumbs
1 tblp. butter

Directions:
Cook broccoli according to package direction (omit salt). Place drained broccoli in 10-inch square baking pan. Combine mushroom soup, shredded cheddar cheese, milk, mayonnaise and beaten egg. Pour mixture over broccoli. Sprinkle with breadcrumb mixture. Bake uncovered.

Preheat Oven: 350 degrees
Bake: 45 minutes

Note:
To save time, make this ahead. Prepare as directed except for baking. Refrigerate overnight. When ready to serve, bake, uncovered, follow directions in recipe.

Variation:
Substitute cauliflower for broccoli.

FRESH FRUIT DIP

This has a creamy texture and because it is not sweet, the natural flavor of the fruit is not hidden. Thanks Barb for this great dip.

Ingredients:
1 package instant French vanilla pudding
1 12 oz. container frozen whipped topping
1 tblp. Lemon juice

Directions:
Mix pudding according to package directions. Fold in whipped topping. Stir in lemon juice.

Note:
Refrigerate for a couple of hours before serving with fresh fruits.

Variation:
You could substitute instant lemon pudding in place of the vanilla pudding.

CHIP BEEF DIP (WARM)

My sister-in-law Chris started serving this appetizer many years ago. It still is a family favorite especially during the Christmas season.

Ingredients:

1 2.5 oz. Package chip beef (rinsed)   ½ cup milk
2 3 oz. Packages cream cheese   1-cup sour cream
2 tblp. chopped green pepper   ¼ tsp. white pepper
¼ cup chopped onion
1 loaf bread (round or oblong) hollowed out

Directions:

Blend cream cheese and milk. Add remaining ingredients (except bread). Place in double boiler. Heat until all ingredients are blended and mixture is smooth. Place mixture in hollowed out loaf of bread. Use cubed bread from loaf for dipping.

Note:

You will need extra cubed bread so cut up another loaf of bread. If you use pumpernickel for the original bread boat select rye or any of your favorites for the second loaf.

BAKED CRAB SPREAD

A real crowd pleaser and so easy to prepare.

Ingredients:
Group A
8 oz. cooked crabmeat
1 cup shredded Monterey jack cheese
3 oz. package cream cheese
⅓ cup mayonnaise
2 tblp. chopped parsley
1 tsp. horseradish
½ tsp Worcestershire sauce

Group B
2 tblp. butter
¼ cup finely chopped onions
1 cup chopped fresh mushrooms

Directions:
Group A:
Combine all ingredients in a medium bowl

Group B:
Melt butter and sauté with onions and mushrooms. Mix well with Group A. Place in small ovenproof dish. Serve with crackers or French bread rounds

Preheat Oven: 350 degrees
Bake: 15 minutes
Serve with crackers or French bread rounds

Note:
If you prefer to use your microwave cook on high for about five to ten minutes or until mixture starts to bubble around edge of baking dish.

Variation:
If you have guests or family members who are allergic to shellfish, you can substitute imitation crab.

SAUSAGE CHEESE BALLS WITH
SWEET AND SOUR SAUCE

This is a sweet and savory appetizer.

Ingredients:
2 pounds regular breakfast sausage (tube packaged)
1 ½ cups all-purpose baking biscuit mix
4 cups shredded sharp cheddar cheese
½ cup finely chopped onion
½ cup finely chopped celery
½ tsp. garlic powder

Directions:
Mix all ingredients. Form into 1-inch balls. Bake 15 minutes on ungreased cookie sheet until golden brown. Makes about 6 dozen.

Preheat Oven: 375 degrees
Bake: 15 minutes

SWEET AND SOUR SAUCE

1-cup brown sugar packed
2 tblp. Cornstarch
⅔ cup white vinegar

2-13.5 cans pineapple chunks
2 tblp. Soy sauce
1 small green pepper chopped

Directions:
In large saucepan combine: brown sugar and cornstarch. Stir in pineapple, with pineapple liquid, vinegar and soy sauce. Heat to boiling, stirring constantly. Reduce heat. Add cooked sausage cheeseballs. Cover and simmer 10 minutes, stir occasionally. Stir in the chopped green pepper; cover. Simmer until the peppers are tender, about five minutes. Pour into a two-quart casserole dish.

Note:
This can be made a day or two before your party. The longer this sets the better it tastes. Use decorative toothpicks for serving. If you want to have sausage cheese balls ready for another time, you can freeze them uncooked.

MINI HOT DOGS WITH BARBEQUE SAUCE

This is one of those appetizers you can make days before you need it. My sister-in-law Chris made these for Christmas Eve many years ago. It has been enjoyed at many family gatherings.

Ingredients:
2 pounds mini hot dogs
2 medium green peppers chopped
2 medium onions chopped
1 tblp. sugar
1 ½ cup sweet relish
½ cup water

1 28 oz. bottle ketchup
2-4 tsp. liquid hot sauce
½ tsp. crushed red pepper
½ cup vinegar

Directions:
Mix all ingredients (except mini hot dogs) in medium saucepan. Simmer for 20 minutes. Add hot dogs and simmer another 10 minutes.

Note:
If you decide to prepare this ahead of time reheat over medium heat.

Variations:
In place of mini hot dogs, use regular frankfurters and cut into fourths.

SPINACH SQUARES

This is a great appetizer for your vegetarian friends.

Ingredient:

10 oz. frozen chopped spinach
1 tsp. salt
2 eggs beaten
2 tblp. minced onion
1 pound shredded cheddar cheese

1 cup flour
1 tsp. baking powder
1 cup milk
¼ pound margarine melted
2 small cans mushrooms chopped

Directions:

Thaw and thoroughly drain spinach. In large mixing bowl, combine flour, salt and baking powder. Add beaten eggs, milk and melted margarine to flour mixture. Stir in onions, cheese, spinach and mushrooms. Pour into slightly greased 9 x 13 baking pan. Cool slightly after baking and cut into bite size squares.

Preheat Oven: 350 degrees
Bake: 35-40 minutes

SPINACH STUFFED MUSHROOMS

What a great way to start a meal. It's difficult to eat just one or two.

Ingredients:

10 ounce frozen chopped spinach
18-20 large fresh mushrooms
½ cup onion, finely chopped
½ cup bread crumbs
1 egg, beaten

1 tblp. Oil
3 cloves garlic minced
1 tblp. Lemon juice
Salt and pepper to taste

Directions:

Cook spinach according to package direction, drain. Remove stems from mushrooms and chop stems finely. Arrange mushroom tops on a cookie sheet. Add oil to a large frying pan and sauté onion, garlic and mushroom stems. Combine spinach, breadcrumbs, lemon juice, egg and sautéed mushroom mixture. Blend well. Fill mushrooms with mixture (if desired top with raged cheddar cheese).

Preheat Oven: 400 degrees
Bake 10-15 minutes
Serve Hot.

Note:

This appetizer will serve four. You will have to adjust the recipe if serving more than four people.

Variations:

For extra flavor, sauté finely ground sausage with onions, garlic and mushroom stems. Drain off fat before adding other ingredients.

ZUCCHINI APPETIZER

Couldn't be easier than this appetizer. Place all your ingredients in one large mixing bowl, pour into a baking pan and bake.

Ingredients:

3 cups sliced zucchini
½ cup finely chopped onion
2 tblp. Snipped parsley
½ tsp marjoram
Dash of pepper
½ cup oil

1-cup baking mix
½ cup grated Parmesan cheese
½ tsp. salt
½ tsp. sweet basil
½ clove garlic, chopped
4 eggs, beaten

Directions:

Mix all ingredients in large bowl. Pour into greased 13 x 9 inch baking pan; bake. Cool and cut into squares.

Preheat Oven: 350 degrees
Bake: 25 minutes uncovered

Note:

This needs to be served hot.

CREAM CHEESE ORANGE MARMALADE SPREAD

The first time I tasted this was at a party given by the pastor of our church. He had a reputation for preparing the most delicious appetizers as well as serving his guests marvelous dinners. Thank you Rev. Walt.

Ingredients:

8 ounces low fat cream cheese (softened)
½ cup orange marmalade
3 strips crisp bacon

Directions:

In a small bowl, beat softened cream cheese; add orange marmalade, and bacon. Place mixture in food processor. Continue mixing until smooth. Chill 2-3 hours before serving. Spread on wheat thins or cracker of your choice.

CRAB SPREAD

If you like spicy, you will enjoy this appetizer.

Ingredients:

1 pound cooked crab chopped
1 cup medium style salsa
3 scallions finely chopped
2-8 oz. packages cream cheese softened

½ cup light mayonnaise
1 tblp. Cajun seasoning

Directions:

Place all ingredients in a large bowl; mix well. Chill 2 hours. Serve with crackers.

Variations:

You could use imitation crab if you have guests that allergic to shellfish. Try using the hot style salsa in place of medium.

BAGEL SPREAD

This is an excellent spread for bagels or toasted French bread.

Ingredients:
1-cup peanut butter
⅔ cup grated carrots
¼ cup plain yogurt
2-4 tblp. Honey

Directions:
Combine all ingredients and blend in food processor. Process until mixture is smooth.

Note:
This is a doubled recipe; cut in half for smaller amount.

GARLIC AND LEMON HUMMUS

Ingredients:
1-cup chickpeas (drained)
½ cup plain yogurt
2 cloves garlic minced
¼ cup Tahitni sesame paste
⅓ cup fresh lemon juice

Directions:
Puree all ingredients in food processor, process for one minute. Serve on crackers or toasted bread.

Makes approx. 2 cups of hummus.

Variations:
Add a small amount of pesto.

PIZZA DOUGH

There is nothing like homemade pizza. The dough is mixed in a food processor. It doesn't get any easier then this.

Ingredients:

1 package dry yeast
¾ cup + 2 tblp. warm water, divided
2 tsp. sugar

1 tsp. salt
1 tblp. oil
2 ¾ cups flour

Directions:

In a measuring cup dissolve yeast in ¼ cup warm water. Add sugar and let stand for 3 minutes. Place metal blade in processor; add all the flour and salt; process for 10 seconds. With processor running pour yeast mixture through feed tube. Gradually pour in remaining water and oil. Process until dough forms a ball and turns in bowl about 25 times. Let dough stand 2 minutes. Process 15 seconds. Turn into a lightly floured bowl; cover with a towel and let rise in warm place for 45 minutes. Punch down. Roll and shape into a round 12-inch circle. Place on baking sheet that has been brushed with olive oil. Spread with tomato sauce and any other toppings of your choice.

Preheat Oven: 425 degrees
Bake: 20 to 25 minutes

Note:

If you have a pizza stone follow directions for baking.

Variations:

Instead of making one large pizza, divide dough into 4 pieces and made individual servings.

GREEN OLIVE SPREAD

Easy to put together and you probably have the ingredients right in your pantry. Chris thanks for sharing this recipe with me.

Ingredients:
8 oz. cream cheese
½ cup mayonnaise
½ cup toasted chopped walnuts
1 cup green stuffed olives chopped
1 tblp. Liquid from olives

Directions:
Combine all ingredients in a food processor. Process until you have a smooth but not a paste spread. Serve with crackers or on Melba rounds.

Note:
The longer this sets the better the flavor.

CLAMS CASINO

We have a number of couples that enjoy getting together. It could be for a picnic or for a holiday celebration. Thank you Marge for introducing us to a great appetizer.

Ingredients:

3 small cans (6 ½ oz.) minced clams
1 tube Ritz crackers
3 stalks celery, diced
1 stick butter

1 lb. bacon
1 green pepper, diced
1 medium onion, diced

Directions:

Fry bacon until crisp. Remove from frying pan; drain on paper towels. In several tablespoons of bacon fat, sauté onions, peppers and celery. In a separate saucepan, melt butter. Crush tube of crackers, add to butter and mix. Add crackers and butter to vegetables. Drain 2 cans of clams well. Reserve juice from 3rd can and add all 3 containers of clams to cracker and vegetable mixture. Crumble bacon. Add to clam and vegetable mixture; mix well. Season with pepper, garlic salt; pour into a greased casserole dish. Bake until heated through. Serve with crackers.

PREHEAT OVEN: 350 degrees
BAKE: 20 minutes

Note:

This recipe will serve a large party. You can cut it in half for a smaller gathering.

Variations:

Substitute margarine for the butter.

MEXICAN TACO SALAD

If you want to save time in the kitchen, put this together ahead of time and bake it just before your guests arrive. My son-in-law Jeff, who enjoys appetizers, gave this recipe to me to add to my appetizer file.

Ingredients:

1 lb. ground beef
1-tomato soup can of water
16 oz. shredded cheddar cheese
2-8oz. cream cheese, room temperature

1 can tomato soup
1 package Chilio dry mix
Tortilla chips

Directions:

Spread cream cheese on bottom of 13 x 9 inch baking pan. Set aside. Brown ground beef, drain off fat. Add tomato soup water and Chilio dry mix to beef. Pour over cream cheese. Sprinkle cheddar cheese over mixture and bake until cheese is melted, about 15 minutes. Use tortilla chips for dipping.

PREHEAT OVEN: 350 degrees
BAKE: 15 minutes
Ovens vary check for melted cheese.

Note:

Let the salad cool slightly before serving.

Variations:

Substitute ground turkey for the ground beef.

SHRIMP DIP

This is a great recipe that goes together easy.

Ingredients:

1-cup mayonnaise
⅓ cup finely chopped green pepper
1 tblp. Prepared horseradish
⅛ tsp. freshly ground pepper
2-cups finely chopped cooked shrimp

1-cup sour cream
¼ cup chili sauce
¼ tsp. salt

Directions:

Combine all ingredients until well mixed. Cover; chill.
Makes 3 cups. Dip with crackers or Melba toast rounds.

Note:

Make sure you inform your friends or family that there is shrimp in this dip, just in case they are allergic to shellfish.

Variations:

Imitation crab can be used in place of the shrimp.

HOT ARTICHOKE DIP

Artichokes are one of my favorite vegetables especially when I can use them in an appetizer.

Ingredients:

½ cup mayonnaise   ½ cup sour cream
⅓ cup grated Parmesan cheese   ⅛ tsp. hot pepper sauce
1 can (14 oz.) artichoke hearts, drained, and chopped

Directions:

Stir all ingredients until well mixed; spoon into small ovenproof dish. Dip with party crackers.

Bake at 350 degrees for 30 minutes or until bubbly.
Makes 2 cups.

Note:

Use the artichoke hearts that are packed in brine; do not use artichokes in marinate.

WHITE BEAN DIP

This dip is low in calories and fat.

Ingredients:
1 tblp. Lemon juice
2 tblp. Plain nonfat yogurt
2 tblp. Chopped fresh parsley
1 (15 oz.) can cannellini beans,
 rinsed and drained

2 garlic cloves
¼ tsp. hot pepper sauce
½ tsp. freshly ground black pepper

Directions:

In a food processor or blender, combine all ingredients, process until smooth. Chill. Serve with toasted pita bread, corn chips or fresh vegetables.

YIELD: 1-¼ cups

Variations:

Great northern beans can be used in place of the cannellini beans.

BREADS

APPLE BREAD

Looking for a way to use those apples that linger in your fruit basket? Give this bread a try. Warm or cold, it's a winner.

Ingredients:
Group A

¼ lb. margarine	2 eggs
1 cup sugar	1 tsp. vanilla

Group B

2 cups flour	1 tsp. baking powder
¼ tsp. salt	

Group C

1 tsp. baking soda	2 tblp. milk

Group D
2 cups finely chopped apples

Directions:
Combine Group A ingredients and cream well. Combine Group B in a separate bowl stir into creamed mixture. Dissolve soda in milk and add to batter. Mix well. Fold Group D into batter.

Pour into greased 9 x 5 x 3 bread pan

Preheat Oven: 350 degrees
Bake: 1 hour

Variations:
Add half a cup raisins or half a cup chopped nuts to batter.

PUMPKIN NUT BREAD

This has been a family favorite for over 30 years.

Ingredients:

1 cup shortening
2 ¾ cups sugar
3 eggs
3 cups flour
1 tsp. baking powder
1 tsp. nutmeg
1 tsp. soda

1 tsp. allspice
⅛ tsp. salt
1 tsp. cinnamon
2 cups pumpkin
1 tsp. vanilla
1 cup chopped nuts (optional)

Directions:

Cream shortening; add eggs, sugar, mix well. Add dry ingredients to creamed mixture. Add pumpkin and vanilla. Fold in nuts. Pour into two bread pans (greased) or four small bread pans.

Preheat Oven: 350 degrees
Bake: 1 hour

Variations:

Try adding a cup of raisins.

CHALLAH BREAD

A Traditional bread for everyday eating. It makes a rich and flavorful French toast. Use a food processor to mix this bread dough.

Ingredients:

¾ cup warm water, divided
1 package yeast
1 tblp. Sugar
2 ¾ cups flour
1 tblp. Butter or margarine

1 tsp. salt
1 egg
1 egg yolk
2 tblp. Water
Poppy or sesame seeds

Directions:

In a measuring cup, dissolve yeast in ¼ cup warm water. Sprinkle sugar in and let stand 3 minutes. Place blade in bowl; process flour, butter, and salt until blended. With processor running pour yeast mixture through feed tube. With processor running slowly pour in egg and remaining warm water through feed tube. Process until dough forms a ball that turns in bowl 25 times. Let dough stand two minutes. Process until dough turns around 15 times. Turn into lightly floured bowl, cover and let rise in warm place for one hour. Punch down. Divide into three equal parts. Shape each into an 18 inch strand. Braid loosely together. Tuck ends under and place on greased baking sheet (or, for a higher loaf, place in greased 9 x 5 inch pan). Let rise 45 minutes. Combine egg yolk and water. Brush over braid. Sprinkle with seeds.

Bake in a preheated 375-degree oven 30 minutes. Remove and cool on rack.

Variations:

Add half-cup raisins or half cup chopped dates to dough during step three.

ZUCCHINI BREAD

What to do with all of that zucchini my husband Tony plants? Well here is one solution. I have been baking this bread for at least 35 years.

Ingredients:

3 eggs
1-cup vegetable oil
2 cups sugar
3 tsp. vanilla
2 cups grated raw zucchini
1 cup chopped nuts (optional)

3 cups flour
1 tsp. salt
3 tsp. cinnamon
1 tsp. soda
½ tsp. baking powder

Directions:

Combine dry ingredients and set aside. Cream eggs, oil and sugar. Add zucchini and vanilla. Mix until blended. Add dry ingredients and mix well. Add nuts.

Recipe will make 3 small or 2 large loaves. Pour into well-greased pans.

Preheat Oven: 325 degrees
Bake: 1 ¼ hours

Variations:

This is bread where you can add raisins or chopped dates.

ZUCCHINI PINEAPPLE BREAD

I am always looking for ways to use the many zucchini that my husband Tony grows every year. This is very moist bread and freezes well.

Ingredients:

3 eggs
2 cups sugar
2 tsp. vanilla
3 cups flour
1 tsp. baking powder
1 tsp. baking soda

1 cup vegetable oil
2 cups unpeeled grated zucchini
½ cup raisins or chopped dates
1 cup chopped nuts
1 cup well drained crushed pineapple
1 tsp. salt

Directions:

Combine dry ingredients and set aside. Cream eggs until fluffy. Add sugar, vanilla and oil. Mix well. Add zucchini to batter. Fold in dry ingredients, pineapple, raisins (or dates) and nuts. Mix well. Pour into two well-greased and floured 9 x 5 loaf pans.

Preheat Oven: 325 degrees
Bake: 1 hour

Note:

This bread freezes well. Start baking in the fall and have this ready for the holidays.

POTATO ROLLS

You won't be able to stop eating these rolls once you start. Thanks Dottie (Grandma Burgess) for a great recipe.

Ingredients:

1 cup sugar
2 eggs
1 tsp. salt
2 packages dry yeast

⅔ cup shortening
6 cups flour
2 medium potatoes (peeled)

Directions:

Dice potatoes and cook in 1 ½ cups water. Cream eggs and sugar. Add salt. Save 1 cup potato water and melt shortening in water. Mash potatoes well. Add potatoes and shortening water mixture to egg and sugar. Add 2 cups flour and yeast and mix. Add remaining 4 cups flour and mix. Cover. Let rise.

Melt one stick of butter. Roll dough on floured board ¼ inch thick. Cut with 3 inch round cookie cutter. Brush with melted butter. Fold in half and place on greased cookie sheet. Let rise.

Preheat Oven: 375 degrees
Bake: 10-12 minutes.

Brush tops of roll with melted butter.

Yield: 50-60 rolls

Note:

The dough for these rolls does not have to be kneaded. Just combine all ingredients and let rise.

ALMOND APPLESAUCE BREAD

Ingredients:

1 cup sugar
1-cup applesauce
⅓ cup oil
2 eggs
3 tblp. Milk
¼ tsp. nutmeg

2 cups flour
1 tsp. baking soda
½ tsp. baking powder
½ tsp. cinnamon
¼ tsp. salt
¾ cup sliced almonds

TOPPING:
¼ cup brown sugar
½ tsp. cinnamon
¼ cup sliced almonds

Directions:

Combine sugar, applesauce, oil, eggs and milk. Combine dry ingredients in separate bowl. Mix wet and dry ingredients together. Add ¾ cup sliced almonds.

Pour into loaf pans (will make 2 nice-size loaves). Combine topping ingredients and sprinkle on top of loaves. Press lightly into the batter.

Bake at 350 degrees for 30 minutes. Cover lightly with foil and bake an additional 30 minutes, or until tester comes out clean.

ORANGE SWEET ROLLS

I have no idea where or who gave me this recipe. It was hand written on a recipe card. These rolls do not call for yeast. Instead baking powder is used and the result is a wonderful sweet roll that is light in texture.

Ingredients:

4 tblp. Melted butter	½ cup orange juice
½ cup sugar	1 tsp. orange rind
2 ⅔ cup flour	3 tsp. baking powder
1 tsp. salt	6 tblp. Cold margarine
1 ⅛ cup milk	6 tblp. Melted butter
⅓ cup cinnamon sugar	

Directions:

Combine 4 tblp. melted butter, orange juice, sugar, orange rind in small saucepan. Bring to a boil and boil 3 minutes. Pour into a 9 inch round pan; set aside. Combine flour, baking powder, and salt; cut margarine into flour mixture; stir in milk to make soft dough. Knead gently 8-10 times. Roll dough on lightly floured surface into a 12" x 16" rectangle. Brush with 6 tblp. melted butter; sprinkle with ⅓ cup cinnamon sugar. Roll up like a jellyroll. Cut into 1 inch slices and place cut side down in prepared pan. Bake. Turn onto serving plate immediately after removing from oven.

Preheat oven: 450 degrees
Bake: 20-25 minutes

Note:

Inverting the sweet rolls immediately allows the orange glaze to cover the sweet rolls on top as well as on the sides.

Variations:

I have baked these rolls according the recipe. I'm sure you could add ½ cup raisins when sprinkling with the cinnamon sugar.

POPPY SEED BREAD

Holidays bring certain foods that we enjoy. My daughter-in-law Debbie bakes this bread as a gift to family and friends. She gave me the recipe so I could bake it not only for the holidays but also all during the year.

Ingredients:

4 cups flour
Dash salt
2 cups sugar
13 oz. can evaporated milk
½ cup poppy seeds

1 Tblp. baking powder
2 cups vegetable oil
4 eggs
1 tsp. vanilla extract

Directions:

Combine dry ingredients and set aside. Place sugar, oil, evaporated milk and eggs in large mixing bowl. Beal well. Add flour mixture; mix well. Stir in poppy seeds and vanilla. Pour into greased 8 x 4 inch loaf pan.

Preheat Oven: 350 degrees
Bake: 1 hour
Cool before removing from pan

Note:

If you are using small loaf pans, test bread with toothpick inserted in center of bread. Baking time will vary when baking smaller loaves.

SAINT JOSEPH'S BREAD

Whether this bread is just toasted, made into French toast or just plain with some butter, pour a cup of coffee or tea and enjoy. This bread is traditionally baked on the Feast of Saint Joseph.

Ingredients:

2 packages dry yeast
1-cup hot scalded milk
1 tsp. salt
6 cups flour (approx.)
Sesame seeds and egg white

1 cup sugar
½ cup butter
3 eggs
⅓ cup lukewarm water

Directions:

Dissolve yeast in ⅓ cup lukewarm water, in a large bowl. In another bowl, combine sugar, scalded milk, butter and salt. Stir until butter melts. Cool to lukewarm temperature. Add eggs one at a time, beat well after each egg. Blend in yeast mixture. Gradually add 5 ½ cups of flour, beating until smooth. Turn out on floured board and knead in additional ½ cup flour. Continue kneading until smooth and elastic, 18-20 minutes. Place dough in greased bowl and let rise in warm place, about 3 hours or until double in size. Punch down and divide dough into 3 pieces.

Roll each piece into a 36-inch rope. With tip of sharp knife, make 1 inch cuts at 1-inch intervals along one side of rope, beginning at the center and working toward one end. Repeat on opposite side of rope, working from center toward other end. Loosely roll whole rope into one large coil. Place on greased baking sheet. Brush loaf with egg white beaten with 1 tsp. water. Sprinkle top with sesame seeds. Place pan in a warm place in kitchen and let rise until double in size, about 2 hours.

PREHEAT OVEN: 350 degrees
BAKE: 20-25 minutes until nicely browned.

Note:

I prefer to line baking sheet with parchment paper instead of greasing.

CAKES

TEMPTATION SPICE CAKE

The flavor of this cake brings back fond memories of the spice cake my mom baked.

Ingredients:

2 cups flour
3 ½ tsp. baking powder
1 tsp. cinnamon
¼ tsp. ground cloves
½ cup shortening
1 tsp. vanilla

1 ⅓ cup sugar
1 tsp. salt
½ tsp. nutmeg
1-cup milk
3 eggs

Directions:

Sift together dry ingredients in large mixing bowl. Add shortening, milk and vanilla. Beat 2 minutes on medium speed. Add eggs and continue beating another 2 minutes until well blended. Pour into two greased and floured 9 inch round cake pans. Cool before frosting.

Preheat Oven: 350 degrees
Bake 30-35 minutes

Variations:

Frost this cake with Cream Cheese Frosting. See recipe.

SOUR CREAM POUND CAKE

This is a great cake to use for strawberry shortcake. Thanks Elly for sharing this great pound cake.

Ingredients:

1-cup margarine
6 eggs
2 ¾ cup sugar
3 cups flour
½ tsp. salt

½ tsp. baking powder
1 cup diary sour cream
½ tsp. lemon extract
½ tsp. orange extract
½ tsp. vanilla extract

Directions:

Beat margarine until creamy. Gradually add sugar. Beat until light and fluffy. Add eggs one at a time. Beat one minute after each egg. Beat two minutes longer. Sift together flour, salt and baking powder. Add to creamed mixture, alternating with the one-cup sour cream. Add extracts until blended. Pour into a greased and floured tube pan. Cool before removing from tube pan.

Preheat Oven: 350 degrees
Bake: 1 ½ hours

Note:

For a great dessert, slice cake and top with your favorite ice cream. Dust the dessert with confectionery sugar.

Variations:

Remove the cooled pound cake from the cake pan, place on a cake dish and drizzle with a lemon or vanilla glaze.

CHOCOLATE ZUCCHINI CAKE

This is another use for the extra zucchini that comes from our garden.

Ingredients:

2 ½ cup flour
2 ½ tsp. baking powder
1 ½ tsp.baking soda
¾ cup butter
3 eggs
2 cups shredded zucchini

½ cup cocoa
1 ½ tsp. salt
2 cups sugar
2 tsp. grated orange rind
1 cup chopped nuts
½ cup milk

Directions:

Sift dry together and set aside. Cream butter and sugar until well blended. Add one egg at a time. Beat well after each egg. Add orange rind and zucchini. Beat well. To the creamed mixture alternate dry ingredients with milk. Fold in nuts. Pour into a greased and floured bunt or tube baking pan. Cool in pan for 15 minutes.

Preheat Oven: 350 degrees
Bake: One hour

Variations:

Drizzle a vanilla glaze on cake.

BANANA SPLIT CAKE

When bananas go on sale buy extras and bake this quick and easy dessert. This recipe goes back at least forty-five years. The only memory I have is that a co-worker named Alice gave it to me.

Ingredients:
1 Yellow cake mix
1 package instant vanilla or banana cream pudding
1-20 oz. can crushed pineapple (drained)
5-8 bananas sliced (do not use over ripe bananas)
1-12 oz. container whipped topping (thawed)

Directions:
Bake cake, according to directions, in a 13 x 9 inch pan. Cool cake completely in baking pan. Mix instant pudding according to directions. Spread pudding on top of cake. Spoon crushed pineapple over pudding. Arrange bananas over pineapple. Frost cake with whipped topping. Keep refrigerated before serving.

Note:
It is important that this cake be served chilled.

Variations:
You could use canned cherry pie filling in place of the pineapple. But I feel the pineapple topping has the best flavor.

CARROT CAKE

My sister-in-law Rita shared her recipe for this wonderful cake with our family. The cream cheese frosting is a must for this cake.

Ingredients:
2 ¼ cup flour
2 tsp. baking soda
2 cups sugar
4 eggs
1 ½ cup chopped nuts

2 tsp. salt
2 tsp. cinnamon
1 ½ cup Crisco oil
3 cups coarsely chopped carrots

Directions:
Sift dry ingredients together and set aside. Combine sugar, oil and eggs. Beat at medium speed for two minutes. Add dry ingredients to creamed mixture. Stir carrots and nuts into batter. Spread into a greased and floured 13 x 9 x 2 inch baking pan.

Preheat Oven: 300 degrees
Bake: About one hour or until tested with a toothpick comes out clean.

Variations:
Frost this cake with a cream cheese frosting. See recipe.

CHOCOLATE CAKE

This has to be the best chocolate cake ever. My aunt Ramona gave this recipe to me. I have been baking this cake for the past 40 years. It's quick and you have all the ingredients in your pantry.

Ingredients:

1 cup sugar
⅓ cup baking cocoa
1 tsp. vanilla
1 tsp. baking soda
⅓ cup vegetable oil

1 ½ cup flour
1 tsp. vinegar
½ tsp. salt
1-cup **cold water**

Directions:

Sift together sugar, flour and cocoa into an ungreased 8 x 8 inch square baking pan. Smooth flour mixture with back of a spoon. Make 5 holes in flour mixture placing vanilla, vinegar, baking soda, salt and oil each in a different hole. Pour the cold water over ingredients and mix with a metal spoon until well blended. After cake has cooled, dust with confectionery sugar.

Preheat Oven: 350 degrees
Bake: 30-35 minutes

Note:

Clean up is quick with this cake because you mix all the ingredients in the pan it is baked in. Also, because this cake has no eggs or milk, it is a wonderful dessert for friends or family who have allergies. I often just dust the cake with confectionery sugar, but a chocolate frosting could also be used.

Variations:

You can't make this any better.

MONKEY BREAD COFFEE CAKE

This is a great cake to have your younger children or grandchildren help assemble. Let them roll the biscuits in the cinnamon sugar and help place the biscuits in the bunt pan.

Ingredients:

4 packages ready to bake biscuits ½ cup margarine
1-cup brown sugar 1 cup chopped nuts

Directions:

Cut biscuits into fourths. Place chopped nuts in the bottom of greased bunt pan. Make a mixture of granulated sugar and cinnamon. Place in a gallon size zip lock bag. Shake biscuits in mixture. Layer all biscuits in bunt pan. Boil half-cup margarine and one-cup brown sugar for one minute. Pour over biscuits and bake. Cool two minutes. Invert coffee cake onto a cake platter.

Preheat Oven: 350 degrees
Bake: 25-30 minutes

Note:

You can pull this cake apart with your hands or use a knife to cut and serve.

DIRT CAKE

Because of the title of this cake, you must be curious as to what exactly does this cake consist of. Debbie, my daughter-in-law is always experimenting. She served this at a family dinner. Watch your guest's faces when you serve this great cake to them.

Ingredients and Directions:
Part I:
In a blender crumble a 20 oz. package Oreo cookies. Divide into 3 parts.

Part II:
Mix, 2 small packages dark chocolate instant pudding with 3 ½ cups milk. Mix, 2 small packages vanilla instant pudding with 3 ½ cups milk.

Part III:
Mix together: 12 oz. cream cheese, 1 cup confectionery sugar, 12 oz. container cool whip.

ASSEMBLE: In a 10 inch clay pot lined with plastic wrap.

LAYERS:
Crumbs
Vanilla pudding
Chocolate pudding
Cream cheese cool whip mixture

Repeat this process ending with crumbs on top.

Note:
Now, the fun part. To present this cake, place a small bouquet of silk flowers in the center of the pot. Purchase a small trowel you would use for gardening and use the trowel to serve the cake. I guarantee you will get raves when you serve this fun cake.

Variations:
The only suggestion I have would be changing the type of flowers you place on the cake.

BANANA CAKE

This is my daughter Joanne's favorite birthday cake.

Ingredients:

2 ½ cups flour
½ tsp. baking soda
½ cup shortening
2 eggs
1 cup mashed banana

2 ½ tsp baking powder
½ tsp. salt
1 ¼ cup sugar
2 tsp. vanilla
¼ cup milk

Directions:

Combine dry ingredients and set aside. Cream shortening and sugar until light and fluffy. Add eggs one at a time; beating thoroughly after each egg. Add vanilla. Add dry ingredients alternate with milk and banana. Mix only to blend; do not over beat. Pour into 2-9 inch greased round cake pans.

Preheat Oven: 375 degrees
Bake: 25 minutes

Test by inserting toothpick in center

Note:

Do not use green bananas. Using ripped bananas adds to the flavor of the cake. Frost cake with White Frosting. See recipe.

CANDY

PEANUT BRITTLE (MICROWAVE)

This is a unique recipe because you cook this in the microwave. I bet you will never purchase peanut brittle again once you have made your own.

Ingredients:

1-cup sugar
⅛ tsp. salt
1½ cups salted party peanuts
1 tblp. Margarine

½ cup light corn syrup
1 tsp. vanilla
1 tsp. soda

Directions:

Line a cookie sheet with aluminum foil. Grease foil with margarine. In a medium size glass bowl, mix sugar, light corn syrup and salt. Cook at full power in microwave 5 minutes. Remove from microwave and stir in peanuts. Cook at full power in microwave 3-5 minutes until mixture turns a light brown. Remove from microwave and stir in margarine, vanilla and soda. Pour brittle mixture on foil and spread with a metal spoon. Let set in cool place. Cool completely. Peel candy off foil and break into pieces.

Note:

When removing mixture from microwave, be careful mixture is very hot. After brittle has been spread on cookie sheet, place-mixing bowl in hot soapy water to remove sticky sugar mixture.

Variation:

Use salted cashews in place of party peanuts.

WHITE TRASH

Once you taste this snack, you will have a hard time leaving it alone. During the years that I worked for a chiropractor, patients would bring baked goods, home-grown fruits and their favorite holiday snacks for the staff. One of our patients, Donna, brought this great candy/snack one Christmas.

Ingredients:
2 cups each of the following:

Rice Chex

Rice Krispies

Salted cocktail peanuts

2 pounds white chocolate wafer

Corn Chex

Cheerios

Stick pretzels (broken into pieces)

2 tblp. Vegetable oil

Directions:
Line two 13 x 10 inch cookie sheets with aluminum foil. Rub cookie sheets with margarine.

Mix cereals, peanuts and pretzels in a very large bowl. In microwave, melt white wafers and oil. Cook at full power and stir every minute until mixture is smooth. Pour over cereal mixture. Mix well. Divide mixture in half spread, with spatula, onto cookie sheets. Let mixture dry in a cool place. Break into pieces and store in sealed container in a cool place.

Note:
Spread the mixture as thin as possible.

Variations:
The only substitute I have made is using salted cashews in place of the cocktail peanuts.

NEVER FAIL FUDGE

I am sure this fudge has been made over and over again. But have you every found yourself wanting to make it and couldn't remember all the ingredients you need without going to the grocery store and reading the back of a marshmallow cream jar. These are the ingredients you need!

Ingredients:

3 cups sugar
⅔ cup evaporated milk
7 oz. jar marshmallow crème
1 tsp. vanilla

¾ cup margarine
12 oz. package chocolate chips
1 cup chopped nuts (optional)

Directions:

Combine sugar, margarine and evaporated milk in heavy 3-quart saucepan, bring to a full rolling boil, stirring constantly. Continue boiling 5 minutes over medium heat, stirring constantly to prevent scorching. Remove from heat; stir in chocolate chips until melted. Add marshmallow crème, nuts and vanilla; beat until well blended. Pour into greased 13 x 9 inch baking pan. Cool at room temperature; cut into squares.

Note:

Make sure air bubbles are not mistaken for a rolling boil. Be patient and watch for rolling boil.

Variations:

If you enjoy walnuts, you could press walnut halves on top of fudge.

COOKIES

CHOCOLATE PIXIES

My daughter Joanne and her childhood friend, Martha, would take over my kitchen to bake these cookies. The only problem was they always ate half the batter and just a few cookies where baked. They would say it was just like eating fudge.

Ingredients:

4 (1-ounce) envelopes premelted unsweetened chocolate

¼ cup butter	2 cups all purpose flour
2 tsp. baking powder	½ tsp. salt
2 cups sugar	3 eggs
½ cup chopped walnuts	Confectioners' sugar

Directions:

In large saucepan melt chocolate and butter over low heat, stirring constantly. Remove from heat. Cool slightly, stir in remaining ingredients, expect confectioners' sugar. Blend well. Chill at least 30 minutes. Shape into balls using a rounded teaspoon for each cookie. Roll in confectioners' sugar, place on greased cookie sheet.

Preheat Oven: 300 degrees
Bake: 18-20 minutes. Cool.

Note:

It is necessary to use a large saucepan in order to hold all the ingredients.

Variations:

I have never changed this recipe.

PUMPKIN COOKIES

These cookies are great because of their size. This cookie will become a favorite with your family.

Ingredients:

3 ½ cups flour
1 ¾ tsp. baking soda
1 ½ tsp. salt
3 ½ sticks butter, softened
1 ¾ cups packed brown sugar
2 large eggs
1 ⅓ cups chopped walnuts

2 ⅓ cups quick oats
2 tsp. ground cinnamon
1 ¾ cups sugar
1 15 oz. can pure pumpkin
1 ¾ tsp. vanilla extract
1 ⅓ cups raisins

Directions:

Mix flour, oats, baking soda, cinnamon and salt in medium bowl. Beat butter, sugar and brown sugar in large bowl until light and fluffy. Add pumpkin, eggs and extract; mix well. Gradually add flour mixture; mix well. Stir in nuts and raisins.

Drop ¼ cup dough onto greased baking sheet; spread into 3-inch circle. Repeat with remaining dough. Bake. Cool on baking sheets for 2 minutes; remove to wire racks to cool completely.

Preheat Oven: 350 degrees
Bake: 14-16 minutes or until
Firm and lightly browned.

Variation:

Decorate with a drizzle of vanilla glaze.

COCONUT WITH DATES

This is a quick and easy cookie. I first tasted this cookie at the monthly gathering of my card group. Thank you Rose for sharing this recipe.

Ingredients:
2 cups flaked coconut
2 cups chopped dates
2 cups chopped walnuts
1 can sweeten Condensed Milk

Directions:
Combine all ingredients; drop by teaspoonful onto a cookie sheet that has been lined with parchment paper.

Preheat Oven: 350 degrees
Bake: 10-12 minutes

Note:
The use of parchment paper will prevent the cookies from burning.

Variation:
Use chopped pecans in place of the walnuts.

PEANUT BUTTER COOKIES

This was an old time favorite of my children. Sunday afternoons were spent baking cookies to be packed in their lunches.

Ingredients:

2 ½ cups flour
1 ½ tsp. baking soda
½ cup shortening
1-cup peanut butter
1 cup brown sugar (packed)

1 tsp. baking powder
½ tsp. salt
½ cup butter
1-cup sugar
2 eggs

Directions:

Combine dry ingredients and set aside. Cream shortening, butter, peanut butter, sugar, brown sugar and eggs mix well. Add dry ingredients to batter. Chill dough 30 minutes. Roll into walnut size balls and place 3 inches apart on ungreased cookie sheet. Flatten with fork that has been dipped in flour. Make a crisscross design on cookie.

Preheat Oven: 375 degrees
Bake: 10-12 minutes

Bake until set but not hard.
Yield: about 6 dozen

Note:

Do not over bake these cookies.

Variations:

Instead of creamy peanut butter try using crunchy. For an added flavor, mix in ½ cup mini-chocolate chips to the finished batter. Baking time will not change.

CHOCOLATE CHIP COOKIES

When my children were growing up this had to be their favorite cookie. My son Vince still eats them right out of the freezer. I can't remember him eating them any other way.

Ingredients:

3 ½ cups flour
1 tsp. salt
⅔ cup shortening
1 cup granulated sugar
2 eggs

1 tsp. baking soda
⅔ cup margarine
1-cup brown sugar (packed)
2 tsp. vanilla
12 oz. mini-chocolate chips

Directions:

Combine dry ingredients and set aside (except chocolate chips). Cream together shortening, margarine, sugars, eggs and vanilla; add dry ingredients to batter. Mix well. Stir in mini-chocolate chips. Drop by rounded teaspoonfuls, about 2 inches apart on ungreased cookie sheet. Bake until delicately brown. Cookies should be still soft. Cool slightly before removing to a cooling rack.

Preheat Oven: 375 degrees
Bake: 8-10 minutes
Yield: about 6 dozen

Note:

I have found, after many years of baking this cookie, you need to beat the batter for at least 4-5 minutes before adding the dry ingredients.

Variations:

Try adding half cup chopped nuts to batter. In place of mini-chocolate chips, use regular size chips.

SUGAR COOKIES

This is not your typical soft dough sugar cookie. It is crisp and buttery and goes great with a cup of tea or a cold glass of milk.

Ingredients:

½ lb. soft margarine
1-cup powder sugar
2 eggs
4 ½ cups flour
1 tsp. cream of tarter

1-cup sugar
1 cup canola oil
2 tsp. vanilla extract
1 tsp. baking powder

Directions:

Combine dry ingredients and set aside. Cream together the margarine, sugar, powder sugar, oil, eggs and vanilla. Add dry ingredients to batter. Mix well to form soft dough. CHILL 1-1 ½ hours. Roll into walnut size balls. Place on ungreased cookie sheet. Dip the bottom of a drinking glass into water then into granulated sugar and flatten balls slightly. Cool cookies on cookie rack.

Preheat Oven: 400 degrees
Bake: 8-10 minutes
Yield: approximately 5 dozen

Note:

Do not over bake cookies. Bake until lightly browned.

Variations:

Substitute almond extract for the vanilla or butter for the margarine. Always use pure extract for these cookies. At Christmas use colored sugars to flatten balls.

ITALIAN MEATBALL COOKIES

Do not be alarmed. This recipe does not contain ground meat. Because of all the spices and ingredients in this cookie, thus the name meatball. I think I have been baking this cookie for over 40 years. This has to be my daughter Joanne's and son Tony's favorite cookie at Christmas.

Ingredients:

1 cup shortening
3 eggs
2 tsp. vanilla extract
5 cups flour
1 tblp. cinnamon
1 tblp. nutmeg
1 cup chopped walnuts

1 ½ cup sugar
1 cup milk
5 tsp. baking powder
1 tblp. cloves
¾ cup baking cocoa
1 cup mini chocolate chips
1 cup chopped dates

Directions:

Combine dry ingredients including spices and set aside. Cream shortening and sugar; add eggs, then milk and vanilla a little at a time. Add dry ingredients to batter and mix thoroughly. Stir in walnuts, chocolate chips and dates. Roll batter into walnut size balls. Place on ungreased cookie sheet. After cookies have cooled, coat them with vanilla glaze. See Vanilla Glaze Frosting recipe.

Preheat Oven: 375 degrees
Bake: 10-13 minutes

Note:

Cookies will form small cracks while baking this is normal. Do not under bake.

Variations:

In place of dates you could substitute raisins. My personal favorite is the chopped dates.

CUTOUT COOKIES

I know what you are thinking, "Another cutout cookie recipe." Try this one. It is by far the best recipe I have every made. When a holiday calls for cookies to be shaped into hearts, shamrocks, bunnies, Christmas trees, bells or just a round circle, this is the recipe to use.

Ingredients:

½ cup shortening   ½ cup margarine
4 cups flour   ½ tsp. salt
2 eggs   1 cup sugar
¼ cup milk   2 tsp. vanilla extract
1 tsp. baking soda

Directions:

In a large mixing bowl cut shortening and margarine into flour as you would for a pastry; and add salt. In a small bowl combine eggs and sugar and mix well. Combine milk, vanilla and soda; add to egg mixture. Add wet ingredients to flour mixture and mix well to form a soft dough. Roll out ¼ inch thick and cut with fancy cookie cutters. Place on ungreased cookie sheets and bake in preheated oven. Cookies should be lightly brown. Frost with your favorite frosting or decorate with colored sugar before baking.

Preheat Oven: 400 degrees
Bake: 10-12 minutes

Note:

Ovens vary in temperature. Check cookies; bake to lightly brown to prevent burning.

Variations:

If you are adventurous substitute other extracts for flavor. BUT the vanilla flavor is by far the best.

TOASTED ANISE BISCOTTI

This cookie is always a favorite in an Italian home. Pour a cup of coffee and start dunking.

Ingredients:

¼ cup butter (no substitute) softened
3 eggs
2 ½ cups Cake Flour
¼ tsp. salt

1-cup sugar
1 tblp. Anise extract
2 tsp. baking powder

Directions:

Cream butter and sugar; add eggs one at a time; beating well after each egg. Add extract. Add combined dry ingredients to creamed batter; mix well. Spread half the batter onto a baking sheet lined with parchment paper; forming an 11-inch x 5-inch rectangle. Repeat with remaining batter on a second sheet. Bake. Cool; remove from baking sheet cut into one-inch slices. Place cut side down on baking sheets. Bake 12-15 minutes long or until browned on each side. Cool on wire racks.

Preheat Oven: 350 degrees
Bake: 15 minutes
Yield: about 2 dozen

Note:

When baking cut slices turn cookies over after first seven minutes of baking. You must use cake flour when making this cookie.

Variations:

Almond extract is a great substitute for the vanilla flavoring.

PIZZELLE (PLAIN)

It is worth investing in a Pizzelle griddle to make these cookies. This cookie is thin and crispy.

Ingredients:

6 eggs	3 ⅓ cup flour
1½ cups sugar	1-cup margarine melted and cooled
4 tsp. baking powder	2 tblp. Vanilla extract

Directions:

Beat eggs, adding sugar gradually, beating until smooth. Add cooled melted margarine and vanilla extract. Sift flour and baking powder and add to egg mixture. (Dough will be sticky enough to be dropped by spoon onto Pizzelle griddle.) Follow directions that come with your machine. Remove cookies from griddle and cool on wire racks.

Note:

Don't get discouraged if first Pizzelle burn. This is normal. Cookies will be lightly brown.

Variations:

Another extract that you can try is anise flavoring. Also, try rolling the cookies around the handle of a wooden spoon as soon as you remove them from the griddle. Then fill them with custard filling or with ice cream for a fancy dessert. Sprinkle with confectionery sugar.

PIZZELLE (CHOCOLATE)

The chocolate Pizzelle is similar to the plain. Directions are exactly the same for this cookie as for the plain Pizzelle.

Ingredients:

6 eggs
2 cup sugar
4 ½ tsp. baking powder
½ cup cocoa.

3 ½ cup flour
1 cup margarine melted and cooled
2 tblp. Vanilla extract

Directions:

Beat eggs, adding sugar gradually, beating until smooth. Add cooled melted margarine and vanilla. Sift flour, baking powder and cocoa and add to egg mixture. (Dough will be sticky enough to be dropped by spoon onto Pizzelle griddle.) Follow directions that come with your machine. Remove cookies from griddle and cool on wire racks.

Note:

Remember first cookies will probably look burned. Continue to spoon batter onto griddle.

Variations:

In place of one tablespoon of vanilla use one-tablespoon orange extract.

JAM FILLED ITALIAN COOKIE

This cookie is Italian all the way. My mother-in-law, Josephine, was the master baker of these cookies. Her homemade grape jam, made from the grapes Pa grew, made the difference. These are still a favorite of her five sons.

Ingredients:

6 eggs
½ cup shortening
4 ¾ cup flour

1 ½ cup sugar
½ cup milk
6 tsp. baking powder

Directions:

Combine flour and baking powder and set aside. Cream eggs, sugar, shortening and milk. Add flour to batter. Add more flour if dough is sticky. (Flour hands when rolling cookies.) Roll into balls, shape of a walnut. Place on ungreased cookie sheets; until lightly brown. Cool on wire rack. Cut in half and fill with grape jam, not grape jelly. Frost cookies with a thin vanilla glaze. See Vanilla Glaze Frosting recipe.

Preheat Oven: 400 degrees
Bake: 10-15 minutes

Note:

Do not over bake. Cookies should be baked to lightly brown.

Variations:

I wouldn't even try to change this recipe.

CRISPY PECAN LOGS

This is a wonderful cookie to make for special occasions and for all holidays.

Ingredients:

2-cup flour	½ tsp. salt
½ cup non-fat dry milk	⅓ cup powdered sugar
½ cup shortening	½ cup soft butter
2 tblp. Vanilla	¼ cup water
1 cup finely chopped pecans	1 cup sifted powdered sugar

Directions:

Sift and place dry ingredients in large mixing bowl. Add shortening, butter, vanilla and water. Beat on low speed until well blended. Stir in nuts. Shape into 2 ½ inch logs. Bake near center of oven until lightly brown. Remove from cookie sheets; while warm roll in 1 cup sifted powdered sugar. Set on wire rack to dry.

Preheat Oven: 375 degrees
Bake: 10-12 minutes
Yield: About 3 dozen

Note:

After cookies dry; roll a second time in powdered sugar.

Variations:

You could substitute finely chopped walnuts for the pecans.

PUMPKIN BARS

I have served these pumpkin bars to my card club and at family gatherings. Each time I get requests for the recipe. Personally, I think it is the Cream Cheese Frosting that makes these a hit.

Ingredients:

2-cup flour	2 tsp. baking powder
2 tsp. cinnamon	1 tsp. baking soda
¼ tsp. salt	1-15 oz. can pumpkin
4 eggs	1 cup oil
1 ⅔ cup sugar	¾ cup chopped pecans (optional)

Directions:

Stir dry ingredients together and set aside. Beat together in a large mixing bowl; eggs, pumpkin, sugar and oil. Mix well. Add dry ingredients; beat until well blended. Stir in pecans. Spread batter in an ungreased 15 x 10 x 1 inch-baking pan. Bake until toothpick inserted comes out clean. Place on cooling rack; frost with Cream Cheese Frosting. See recipe.

Preheat Oven: 350 degrees
Bake: 25-30 minutes

Makes: 24 bars

Note:

Because of the amount of batter, it is necessary that you use the recommended 15 x 10 x 1 inch pan for these bars.

Variations:

I have never varied this recipe.

LEMON ITALIAN COOKIES

My mom was born in Canada. Years after she arrived in our hometown her dear friend Rose gave this recipe to our family. It became a tradition to serve these cookies at Easter.

Ingredients:

¼ lb. butter   ½ cup + 2 Tblp. sugar
3 eggs   ¼ tsp. salt
¼ cup milk   2 Tblp. pure lemon extract
3 ½ cups flour   2 Tblp. + 1 tsp. baking powder

Directions:

Combine dry ingredients and set aside. Cream butter and sugar well. Add eggs one at a time. Add milk and lemon extract. Gradually add dry ingredients to wet mixture. Mix well. Roll into the size of a walnut. Place on greased baking sheet or line baking sheet with parchment paper. Cool completely before frosting cookies. See glaze-frosting recipe.

Preheat Oven: 400 degrees
Bake: 8-10 minutes
Yield: Approx. 4 dozen

Note:

Do not bake these cookies until they are golden brown. If they are over baked it will cause them to be very dry.

Variations:

You could substitute margarine for the butter. Also, pure vanilla extract can replace the lemon. Use lemon extract in the frosting for extra lemon flavor.

ALMOND NUT BISCOTTI

These store well in the freezer and are ready when friends or family drop in for a visit. Brew a pot of coffee and enjoy.

Ingredients:

5 eggs
1-cup sugar
1 Tblp. baking powder
1 cup sliced roasted almonds

3 ½ cups flour
½ cup oil
2 Tblp. pure almond extract
½ tsp. salt

Directions:

Place all dry ingredients into a large mixing bowl (including almonds). Mix and make a well in the center. Place all wet ingredients into the well and stir to incorporate the dry ingredients until you form soft dough. Place dough onto a well-floured board and knead until dough is smooth. Flour the board as necessary so dough is not sticky. Form into a thick log and divide into 6 portions. Roll each portion into rope about the thickness of a quarter coin. Roll each log 11-½ inches long. Place on greased baking sheet or line baking sheet with parchment paper. Pat rope with your hand until the dough is about 2 inches wide. Brush with an egg wash. Bake and cool.

Cut into ¾ inch slices on the diagonal. For toasting, place on same cookie sheet, cut side down and toast in a 375 degree oven for about 8 minutes.

Preheat Oven: 350 degrees
Bake: 20 minutes

Note:

To make an egg wash: beat l egg with 1 tsp. water.

Variations:

Substitute pure anise extract for the almond flavoring.

FINGER SANDWICH BUTTER COOKIES

The traditional Italian wedding cookie cake will always have these butter cookies.

Ingredients:

¾ lb. butter
1 ½ eggs*
1 ¼ tsp. baking powder
Finely chopped nuts
Jam (about 8 oz. jar)

1 cup sugar
3 ¼ cups flour
2 ½ tsp. vanilla
Coconut

*To measure ½ an egg, beat a whole egg with a fork. Measure off 1 ½ Tblp. This is equivalent to ½ an egg.

Directions:

Preheat oven at 350 degrees. Cream butter and sugar; add eggs and vanilla. Add dry ingredients. Mix well. Using star tip #4 "S" tube, pipe out in 2-inch bars on greased baking sheet.

Bake at 350 degrees for about 5-7 minutes. Cool.

Put baked cookies together with jam. Dip one end in jam then in coconut. Can also dip in melted chocolate (3 oz. chocolate chips melted with 3 Tblp. margarine) then dip in chopped nuts or leave some plain with just the chocolate.

Yield: Approx. 80 cookies

Note:

Seedless raspberry jam is the best jam for putting these cookies together.

Variations:

Can also dust some of the cookies with confectionery sugar or put the cookies together with melted chocolate instead of the jam.

BELGIAN BUTTER COOKIE

My sister-in-law Frances moved to Canada after marrying. She is an excellent baker. During one of our visits at her home, she served this cookie. Because I have a passion for baking top quality cookies, she shared this one with me.

Ingredients:

2 ½ cups flour
1 tsp. cream of tarter
1-cup butter soft
1 egg

1 scant tsp. baking soda
¾ cup sugar
2 tsp. vanilla
Raspberry Jam

Directions:

Sift flour, baking soda and cream of tarter and set aside. Cream until fluffy, butter and sugar; add egg and vanilla. Gradually add flour mixture to creamed mixture. Form into a ball. CHILL 30 minutes. Divide dough into ¼'s. Roll on floured board ¼ inch thick, cut with 2 inch round cookie cutter. Place on ungreased cookie sheet. Bake. Cool on rack. Place ¼ tsp. raspberry jam on one cookie, assemble with another cookie (sandwich style).

Place a small amount of vanilla glaze in center of cookie. Top with a small piece of maraschino cherry.

Preheat Oven: 350 degrees
Bake: 7 minutes until lightly brown.

Note:

I suggest you line cookie sheets with parchment paper. Saves on cleaning and cookies bake evenly.

Variations:

Instead of making sandwich style cookies, I have just glazed the cookies individually.

ALMOND MACAROONS

Italian bakeries have great cookies, but you can't compare bakery cookies to homemade almond macaroons. You must use the almond paste that is found in Italian stores.

Ingredients:

2 cups almond paste**
½ cup egg whites
1 tsp. pure orange extract
Maraschino cherries

2 cups confectionery sugar
1 tsp. pure almond extract
Sliced almonds

Directions:

Almond paste needs to be room temperature. With hands or use an electric mixer, work in egg whites in paste until smooth. Add confectionery sugar, orange and almond extracts, working until smooth. Line baking sheets with greased foil. This will prevent cookies from sticking. Squeeze through pastry bag using a #4 "S" star tip. If you don't have a pastry bag, pinch off enough dough to form 1 ½ inch ball; place on baking sheet and flatten slightly with hand. Top with a few slices almonds or top with a piece of maraschino cherry.

Preheat Oven: 325 degrees
Bake: 15-20 minutes until golden brown
Yield: Approx. 50

Note:

**You must use almond paste that is sold in Italian grocery stores. To prevent dough from sticking to your hands, if you hand roll, place a small amount of flour on your hands. Store in a tightly closed container. Cookies can also be frozen.

Variations:

In place of the sliced almonds, I prefer to use pine nuts as a garnish before baking.

FRUIT BARS (CUCCIDATI)

A traditional Italian cookie made for the Christmas holiday. The filling needs time to marinate, so plan ahead when baking this great cookie.

Ingredients:
FILLING:

½ lb. dry figs	½ lb. dates
½ lb. chopped nuts	½ lb. yellow raisins
10 oz. honey	½ tsp. allspice
⅛ tsp. ground cloves	½ tsp. pure orange extract
¼ cup rum	2 tblp. water

Directions:
Grind all fruit using a hand or electric grinder. Mix honey with water and bring to a boil. Remove from heat; add allspice, cloves, rum and extract. Mix with the ground fruit. Place in a covered container for 5 days.

DOUGH:

5 cups flour (1 ½ lbs.)	3 tblp. Baking powder
½ tsp. salt	2 eggs
1 ½ cups sugar	½ cup oil
2 tblp. Pure vanilla extract	½ cup milk

In large bowl mix flour, baking powder and salt. Make a well in center; add eggs, oil, milk, vanilla and sugar. Beat wet ingredients with fork until well mixed; continue mixing flour from the edges. When to thick, finish mixing by hand. Turn onto floured board and knead slightly until dough is smooth. Divide dough into 4 portions. Roll each portion into a rope about 1 ½ inch in diameter. Flatten slightly by hand, then by rolling pin, to about ½ inch thick and 3 inches to 4 inches wide. Fill center with a rope of marinated fruit. Bring up sides of dough around filling and pinch dough closed. Roll rope to even off. Flatten slightly with hands. Cut in 1-¼ inch pieces (resemble small bar). Slash both sides of center bar with knife. Place on greased cookie sheets brush with egg wash (1 egg + 1 tsp. water, beaten well). Sprinkle with confetti candy.

Preheat Oven: 375 degrees
Bake: 10-13 minutes
YIELD: APPROX. 75

DRINKS

FRUIT PUNCH

This is a refreshing fruit punch for any occasion. My grandchildren enjoy this in the summer and it is always made at Christmas time.

Ingredients:
1-12 oz. can frozen orange juice
1-12 oz. can frozen lemonade
1-12 oz. can frozen pink lemonade
1-6 oz. can frozen pineapple juice
1 ½ quarts water
3 quarts ginger ale

Directions:
Mix juices and lemonades with water in large punch bowl. Add ginger ale; add oranges slices and maraschino cherries to punch.

Note:
This recipe can be cut in half if you need to mix punch in smaller batches.

Variations:
Make an ice ring, using oranges, cherries and the juice from the maraschino cherries. This is a great punch if you are having just adults. Then try adding vodka (to taste).

SNEAKY PETE'S (WHISKEY SOUR)

A smooth whiskey sour made in the blender. When my sister-in-law Barb has a party, you can be sure this is ready for you when you arrive.

Ingredients:
1-12 oz. can frozen lemonade
½ can whiskey (use lemonade can)
8-12 ice cubes (crushed before adding to whiskey lemonade mixture)

Directions:
Place all ingredients in a blender, using blend speed, mix until smooth.

YELLOW BIRDS

Be careful of this one. They go down to easy. Thanks Judy for many happy gatherings with friends. Especially after a couple of pitchers of Yellow Birds have been
enjoyed by all.

Ingredients:
2-16 oz. bottles of unsweetened orange juice
1-16 oz. empty orange juice bottle filled with Vodka
3 cans thawed frozen pineapple juice (6 oz. size)
9-12 packets sweetener

Directions:
In a large pitcher, mix all ingredients. Place ice in glasses and fill with drink mixture. Enjoy!

Note:
Do not double this recipe. Mix each pitcher, as you need it.

Variations:
This is great just as it is.

FROSTINGS

CHOCOLATE SOUR CREAM FROSTING

Looking for a rich creamy chocolate frosting? This one is for you.

Ingredients:

12 oz. semi-sweet chocolate chips   ½ cup butter
1-cup (8 oz.) sour cream   1 tsp. vanilla extract
4 ½-5 cups confectionery sugar

Directions:

In a heavy saucepan, melt chocolate chips and butter over low heat. Remove from heat and cool for 5 minutes. Place mixture in a mixing bowl; add sour cream and vanilla. Mix well; add sugar; beat until light and fluffy. Spread between cake layers and over top and sides of cake.

Note:

Be sure to refrigerate before serving and also any leftovers.

Variations:

Can't think of any.

VANILLA PUDDING FROSTING

This is a great change from the run of the mill basic vanilla frosting.

Ingredients:

3 oz. package cooked vanilla pudding
1 cup milk
1 cup granulated sugar

½ cup soft butter
½ cup Crisco shortening

Directions:

In medium saucepan, mix pudding and milk. Cook over medium heat until thick. Place in a bowl and cool in refrigerator until cool, about 45 minutes. Cream butter, sugar and shortening until smooth. Add cooled pudding and beat on medium high speed for 15-20 minutes; until sugar is dissolved. Frost cake. Refrigerate any leftover cake.

Note:

Make sure pudding is completely cooled before adding it to butter mixture. Just a reminder, you must use granulated sugar.

Variations:

This frosting goes great with a banana cake but you can use a chocolate cake as well.

CHOCOLATE CREAM CHEESE FROSTING

This is another great chocolate frosting that will delight family and friends.

Ingredients:

8 oz. cream cheese softened

2 tsp. vanillas extract

1-2 tblp. Milk

½ cup butter softened

6 ½ cups sifted confectionery sugar

⅓ cup unsweetened cocoa powder

Directions:

Beat cream cheese, butter and vanilla until light and fluffy. Gradually add 2 cups confectionery sugar and cocoa, beating well. Gradually beat in remaining sugar until smooth. Beat in milk, if needed, to reach spreading consistency. Add a little milk at a time. Makes about 3 ½ cups.

Note:

Depending on what type of consistency you are looking for to frost a cake, you may adjust the use of the milk. Also, I do not recommend using light or fat free cream cheese.

Variations:

Try using almond extract in place of the vanilla.

CREAM CHEESE FROSTING

This recipe goes great with the Pumpkin Bars in the cookie section. It can also be used with my Carrot Cake recipe.

Ingredients:

3 oz. cream cheese softened
½ cup butter softened

1 tsp. vanilla
2 cup sifted confectionery sugar.

Directions:

Beat cream cheese, butter and vanilla together in a medium bowl until smooth and fluffy. Gradually add the sifted confectionery sugar. Beat until smooth.

Note:

After baked goods have been frosted, keep refrigerated. I do not recommend using light or fat free cream cheese.

Variations:

Don't change a thing.

VANILLA GLAZE FROSTING

This is a great frosting for dipping Italian cookies. You could also use this frosting to glaze a bunt cake.

Ingredients:

½ lb. confectionery sugar
4 to 6 Tblp. milk (approx.)

1 tsp. vanilla extract
1 Tblp. margarine

Directions:

Combine sugar, extract and margarine. Mix well. Add milk a little at a time until consistency you want is reached. Dip tops of cookies in frosting and let dry. Frost approx. 48 cookies.

Note:

This recipe can be doubled depending on how many cookies you need to frost.

Variations:

In place of the margarine, use butter. Substitute lemon extract for the vanilla when you need a lemon frosting.

PINEAPPLE FROSTING

No fuss and goes together easy.

Ingredients:

1-3 oz. package instant vanilla pudding
1-13 ½ oz. can crush pineapple, undrained
1-12 oz. container whipped topping (thawed)

Directions:

Stir pudding into crushed pineapple. Fold into whipped topping. Do not over mix. Frost white, yellow or angel food cake.

Note:

Cake must be refrigerated after frosting.

WHITE FROSTING

This frosting is unique because of the use of granulated sugar. I have been frosting cakes with this frosting for the past 50 years. If you enjoy a frosting that is not sweet, this is the one for you. Aunt Ramona, thank you for this recipe.

Ingredients:

5 tblp. flour   1-cup milk
6 tblp. margarine   6 tblp. shortening
1 cup granulated sugar   1 tsp. vanilla extract

Directions:

Place flour in a medium saucepan; add milk. Cook over medium low heat; cook to form a paste. Stirring constantly. Place cooked paste in glass bowl; cover with plastic wrap, placing plastic wrap directly on paste, and cool in refrigerator. Cream margarine, shortening, granulated sugar and vanilla in large mixing bowl. Add cooled paste and beat well.

Note:

This frosting has the texture of whipped cream. I suggest you refrigerate your cake before serving. The frosted cake tastes the best after being refrigerated.

Variations:

Change this recipe, never.

MEATS

CHICKEN WITH WHITE BAR-B-QUE SAUCE

This is an old recipe that originated with the 4 H club of America. Chicken will be golden brown and has a wonderful flavor. My daughter Joanne brought this great marinate to our barbeques.

Ingredients:

1-cup vinegar
½ cup salad oil (not olive oil)
2 tblp. Poultry seasoning
1-2 lbs. Chicken breasts or chicken parts

4 tsp. salt
½ tsp. white pepper
1 egg

Directions:

Place ingredients in a blender and mix until fluffy in consistency. Arrange chicken in a baking pan; marinate in bar-b-que sauce. Refrigerate for at least 1 hour. Place chicken on grill; discard marinate.

Note:

Grill must be medium hot. Be sure to turn chicken frequently so it does not burn.

STUFFED CABBAGE ROLLS

As I started to select the recipes for this cookbook I knew I had to include this one. It is a favorite of my husband and our children.

Ingredients:
12 large cabbage leaves
1 ¼ lb. ground beef
½ tsp. pepper
1 small onion chopped
½ tsp. poultry seasoning
2 tblp. Vegetable oil
1 tblp. Brown sugar

2 tsp. salt
1 cup <u>cooked</u> rice
1 egg
¼ cup water
2-8oz. cans tomato sauce
1 tblp. Lemon juice

Directions:
Place cabbage leaves in large pot, cover with boiling water until limp. Mix together the ground beef, salt, pepper, cooked rice, onion, egg and poultry seasoning. Fill each cabbage leaf with mixture; fold in sides, roll up, fasten with a toothpick. In a large fry pan, heat oil and brown cabbage rolls. Mix together the tomato sauce, brown sugar, lemon juice and water; pour over cabbage rolls. Cover and simmer one hour basting occasionally.

Note:
Make sure your heat is at a low simmer or the cabbage rolls will stick to the bottom of fry pan.

Variations:
To cut down on the fat; try substituting ground turkey for the ground beef. I prefer the beef. Instead of stuffing the cabbage leafs, try stuffing green peppers. Place stuffed peppers in an ovenproof baking dish; pour tomato sauce mixture over peppers. Bake, covered, at 350 degrees for one hour or until peppers are tender.

SLOPPY JOE'S

I know this is available in the grocery store and all you need to do is open a can; heat and serve. Well, if you like a great spicy Sloppy Joe, you will enjoy this one. Marilyn, I think of you each time I make this recipe.

Ingredients:

1 ½ lbs. Ground beef
1 medium green or red pepper
Salt and pepper to taste
2 tblp. Worcestershire sauce
1 tblp. Ketchup

1 medium onion
2-3 tblp. Chili powder
Dash or two of ground red pepper
1 tblp. Barbeque sauce

Directions:

Brown ground beef; add remaining ingredients and simmer for half and hour; stirring occasionally. Serve in a hamburg roll or Kaiser roll.

Note:

Depending on your taste buds, you will have to determine how much ground red pepper to use.

Variations:

Again, you could substitute ground turkey for the ground beef.

PORK TENDERLOIN WITH MARINATE

Fire up your gas grill. When pork tenderloins are on sale stock up and have this dish ready for summer picnics. I tested many combinations of ingredients for this marinate. This one was the best.

Ingredients:
2-3-lbs. pork tenderloin
1-cup lite soy sauce
½ cup white wine (mellow)
Salt and pepper to taste
2 tblp. honey

1 tsp. fresh or ground ginger
½ tsp. sesame oil
2 cloves minced garlic
½ cup apricot preserve

Directions:
Place pork tenderloin in shallow baking pan. Combine rest of ingredients; mix well. Pour over pork tenderloin; cover and marinate at least 4 hours in refrigerator. Heat grill to medium-low. Cook to medium well. Meat should have a trace of pink in center. Last 10 minutes of grilling; brush with warm apricot preserve.

Note:
Do not over cook the pork tenderloin.

Variations:
Try chicken with this marinate. Marinate for only 1 hour.

CHICKEN FRENCH

Thanks to my dear friend Judy, I now can make Chicken French at home. This is one of my favorite dishes when eating out.

Ingredients:
2 large boneless chicken breasts
1-cup flour seasoned with salt and pepper to taste
2 eggs well beaten
2 small shallots chopped or one small onion chopped
2 tblp. Olive oil, plus 2 tblp. butter
½ cup white wine
Juice of ½ lemon

Directions:
Cut chicken breasts into thin slices. Mix together flour, salt and pepper. Dredge the chicken in the flour then into the beaten egg; back into the flour. Set aside. In a medium size fry pan; sauté shallots, or onions, in the olive oil and butter. Remove and set aside. Brown the floured chicken in the oil and butter drippings. Add more oil if needed. Add the white wine and lemon juice to the chicken. Put shallots back into pan with chicken. Simmer about 8 minutes.

Note:
Chicken should be lightly browned before adding remaining ingredients.

Variations:
Judy suggests adding artichoke hearts or fresh mushrooms; just before you start to simmer.

SWISS STEAK

Another recipe created by my mom. I substituted crushed tomatoes with herbs in place of whole tomatoes and added sweet corn. The seasoned flour used to coat the meat makes wonderful brown gravy. My family has enjoyed this dish for many years.

Ingredients:

1 cup flour
¼ tsp. pepper
3-lbs. round steak
2 medium onions sliced
1-20 oz. can crushed tomatoes

1 tsp. salt
½ tsp. paprika
3 tblp. Vegetable oil
1-2 cups water
1 cup canned sweet corn

Directions:

Combine flour, salt, pepper and paprika, set aside. Slice round steak into thin strips approx. 3 inches by 4 inches. Pound seasoned flour on both sides of steak. Heat oil in a large fry pan (do not use Teflon pan). Lightly brown onions in hot oil; remove onions and set aside; brown steak well on each side. Top meat with onions; add tomatoes, add enough water to cover the meat. Using a metal spoon to scrape the bottom of the pan to release the browned flour bites. Add corn. Cover, reduce heat to a simmer; cook at least 1-½ hours. Stirring occasionally. Serve with rice or mashed potatoes. SERVES: 6-8

Note:

Because the flour makes thick gravy, make sure you stir often. If to thick, add more water or use beef broth.

Variations:

If there are any variations to this recipe, I can't think of any.

PASTA

MANICOTTI SHELLS

Homemade pasta is the best. After you fill these shells with your favorite ricotta or meat filled sit back and enjoy.

Ingredients:

1 cup flour
6 eggs

¾ cup + 2 tblp. milk
salt to taste

Directions:

Place flour in mixing bowl; add salt; add milk a little at a time; add eggs one at a time. Beat well after each egg. Mixture will resemble thin crepe batter. Using an 8-inch non-stick fry pan; lightly spray with a non-stick spray. Pour small amount of batter into fry pan, about 4 tablespoons. Roll mixture until bottom of pan is covered. When batter is set, slightly firm, prick with a fork. DO NOT BROWN. Remove from fry pan and place on a small plate; put waxed paper between shells. Fill with your favorite pasta filling. Place filling near outside edge and roll up. Put tomato sauce on bottom of baking dish. Place filled shells in single layer in baking pan. Cover with sauce; sprinkle with grated Parmesan cheese. Cover with aluminum foil. Bake.

Preheat Oven: 350 degrees
Bake: 45-50 minutes

Let stand 5-10 minutes before serving.

Note:

Shells can be made day before; store in refrigerator. Let stand at room temperature while mixing filling. Bake as directed.

RICOTTA GNOCCHI

These are a change from the traditional potato gnocchi. They are lighter in texture.

Ingredients:
2 cups flour
1 ½ cup Whole Milk Ricotta (do not use light or skim milk product)
1 egg
Pinch of salt

Directions:
Place all ingredients in a food processor. Mix 5-10 seconds forming a ball. Place on floured board; knead 2-3 times. Divide into 4 pieces and roll in a rope the size of a nickel. Cut into gnocchi pieces. Place in salted boiling water. Gnocchi are cooked when they rise to the top. Placed on a serving platter. Cover with tomato sauce.

Note:
If you do not have a food processor, place all ingredients in a large mixing bowl and mix by hand.

PASTRIES

FRIED DOUGH

A Christmas Eve tradition in our home. Pronounced in Italian Crispidi Facile. Mom was the expert when it came to making this fried dough. My son Pat is mastering this old family favorite. I have typed this recipe exactly the way my mom wrote it.

Ingredients:
½ yeast cake large size
2 ½ cups flour
½ tsp. salt

Directions:
Melt yeast in 2 cups lukewarm water. Add flour and mix well with a wooden spoon. Cover and let rise half-hour. Add salt, mix again and let rise until double in size. The batter will be soft and sticky. Place about a ¼ cup batter in the palm of your hand and drop into deep hot shortening. (350 degrees). Brown puffs on all sides and drain on absorbent paper towels. Cool and dust with confectionery sugar.

Note:
My mom would say, "When the puffs turn over by themselves, you know the batter is just right."

Variations:
In place of the confectionery sugar, drizzle honey on the plain cooled puffs. Another variation is to add anchovies to batter before dropping into hot shortening. Dry. Do not dust with confectionery sugar.

PLUM KUCHEN

This is a great way to use the Italian plums we harvest at the end of summer. Sandra, because of your German heritage your recipe is enjoyed by my family.

Ingredients:
1 ½ sticks butter
1-cup sugar
2 tsp. vanilla
4 eggs
2 cups flour
3-4 pounds Italian plums (halved) washed and dried
½ cup cinnamon sugar

Directions:
Cream butter and eggs. Add sugar, vanilla and flour. Mix well. Spread in greased 9 x 13 baking pan. Lay plums; cut side up, on batter. Sprinkle with cinnamon sugar before and after baking.

Preheat Oven: 350 degrees
Bake: 30-35 minutes

MINI CHEESECAKES

Enjoy cheesecake without eating a large piece of cake. Thanks to my dear friend Laurie, my family and friends have enjoyed these cheesecakes.

Ingredients:

2 ½ dozen vanilla wafer cookies
2 8 oz. packages cream cheese (lite)   2 eggs
1 tblp. Lemon juice.   1 tsp. vanilla
1 can pie filling, cherry or blueberry   ¾ cup sugar

Directions:

Place vanilla wafer in bottom of small cupcake pan. Use one foil or two paper liners. Mix together cream cheese, eggs, lemon juice, vanilla and sugar until fluffy in texture. Fill cupcake liner with cream cheese mixture. About ¾ filled. Bake. Cool and spoon pie filling over each cheesecake.

Preheat Oven: 375 degrees
Bake: 20 minutes

Note:

You can bake these for any special occasion. A tray served at a bridal shower will get raves.

APPLE CREAM SCONES

My sister-in-law Pauline is from England and has remarked that these are one of the best scones she has tasted. Chop up tart apples, such as Granny Smith for these tender biscuits.

Ingredients:

2 cup chopped tart apple
6 tblp. butter
1 tblp. Instant coffee crystals
1 tsp. hot water
½ cup whipping cream

2 ¼ cup all-purpose flour
⅓ cup sugar
1 tblp. Baking powder
¼ tsp. salt
2 tblp. Coarse sugar

Directions:

Cook apple in 2 tablespoons of butter until tender and liquid is almost evaporated, stirring often; cool slightly. Dissolve coffee in water; stir in cream. Mix flour, ⅓ cup sugar, baking powder, and salt; cut in remaining butter till pieces resemble coarse crumbs. Add apples and coffee mixture; stir just till dough clings together. On a lightly floured surface, knead 6 times. On an ungreased baking sheet pat dough into an 8-inch circle. Top with coarse sugar. Cut into 12 wedges; separate slightly. Bake. Cool slightly; separate. Serve warm.

Preheat Oven: 400 degrees
Bake: 20-25 minutes or till done

Note:

Be sure you separate the wedges slightly before baking. I use Granny Smith apples.

Variations:

Substitute Jonathan apples for the Granny Smith.

SWEET BOWKNOTS (WANDE')

With my mother by my side (in spirit), she guides my hands to roll the dough as thin as possible. It wouldn't be Christmas without this pastry.

Ingredients:

6 large eggs
3 cups flour
¼ tsp. salt
2 tblp. butter
½ cup confectionery sugar

3 tblp. granulated sugar
½ tsp. orange extract
1 tsp. almond extract
3 cups peanut oil for frying

Directions:

Beat eggs lightly; add granulated sugar, salt and extracts; blend thoroughly. Place flour in a large mixing bowl. Cut in butter; add egg mixture. On a floured board knead until a smooth ball is obtained. If dough is too soft gradually add a little flour to make a firm but not hard dough. Set dough aside for 30 minutes. Then cut dough into four sections. Roll on a well-floured board until **wafer-thin.** Cut with pastry cutter into strips 6 inches long by ¾ inch wide. Tie in individual loose knots and fry in deep hot peanut oil 375 degrees until golden brown. Drain on paper towels. Just before serving, sprinkle with confectionery sugar. Makes about 6-7 dozen bowknots.

Note:

In place of peanut oil I have used Crisco shortening. It is important that you roll the dough as thin as possible.

Variations:

Try drizzling honey on fried bowknots before serving.

PECAN CUPS

If you like pecan pie, you will enjoy these pecan cups. These are delicate and a great finger food to serve at parties. Thank you Laurie for sharing this great dessert.

Ingredients:

1-8 oz. package cream cheese
2 ½ cups flour

½ pound butter

2 ½ cups brown sugar
1 tsp. vanilla
Finely chopped pecans

4 tblp. melted butter
3 eggs slightly beaten

Directions:

Combine cream cheese, butter and flour. Use hands to make soft dough. Using mini cupcake pan, roll dough into small balls, filling ½ of cupcake tin. Press dough forming down and up sides of tin. Combine brown sugar, melted butter, vanilla and eggs. Pour into each cup. Sprinkle with chopped pecans. Bake.

Preheat Oven: 350 degrees
Bake: 30 minutes

Remove from oven after 30 minutes even it they don't look completely baked.

Note:

It is important to remove the pecan cups after 30 minutes or they will be to dry.

Variations:

You can substitute finely chopped walnuts in place of pecans.

PIE PASTRY

When it came to making piecrust; my mom was the master. I grew up with this wonderful mother, who only measured 4ft. 11 inches, and measured nothing. When she made her piecrust, it was a handful of flour and a scoop of shortening; then add the cold water. Even though I measure my ingredients, I feel my pastry comes <u>close</u> to hers.

Ingredients:
Pastry for a two crust 9 inch pie
2 ½ cups flour   1 cup shortening
1 ¼ tsp. salt   1 cup cold water-with 3 ice cubes

Directions:
In a one-cup measuring place ice cubes, fill with cold water. Set aside. Combine flour and salt. With a pastry blender cut shortening into flour and salt mixture. With a fork gently mix in water a little at a time. Mix only until dough comes together. Do not over mix. Form into a ball; wrap in plastic wrap and chill in refrigerator until ready to use.

Note:
It is important that you do not over handle this pastry dough.

Variations:
I can't think of one.

CREAM PUFF PASTRY

When asked by friends and family to bring a dessert, this has to be the one that is requested the most. The filling is the secret.

Ingredients:

1-½ cups water   ¾ cup butter (l ½ sticks)
1-½ cups all-purpose flour   6 eggs

Directions:

Heat water and butter to a rolling boil in a saucepan. Stir in flour, stir vigorously over low heat until mixture forms a ball that leaves sides of pan—about one minute. Remove from heat and cool about 10 minutes at room temperature. Place mixture in a mixing machine bowl and beat in eggs thoroughly, ONE AT A TIME. Beat until smooth. (Breaks off when spoon is raised.) Using a pastry bag and #9 plain tube draw out on a lightly greased baking sheet about 2-¼ inches. If you do not have a pastry bag and #9 tube, drop by tablespoon onto baking sheet. Bake. Fill with cream filling. (See cream filling for cream puffs.)

PREHEAT OVEN: 400 degrees
BAKE: 25-30 minutes
Cool before removing from pan.

Note:

I use parchment paper instead of greasing baking sheet. Easy clean up and pastry bakes evenly. I have made the cream puff shells a couple of days before I need them. They freeze well. Take out of freezer at least 2 hours before you fill them. Let them dry at room temperature.

Variations:

No variations for this one.

CREAM FILLING FOR CREAM PUFFS

The use of vanilla and orange extract makes this filling unique.

Ingredients:

1 qt. whole milk
¾ tsp salt
3 eggs
1 tsp. pure orange extract

1-cup sugar
½ cup cornstarch
1 tsp. pure vanilla extract

Directions:

Measure sugar and salt; add to 2 cups milk. Place in saucepan and stir well; bring to a boil on medium heat. Add cornstarch, vanilla, orange extracts; and eggs to the remaining 2 cups milk and mix until well blended with a wire whip. When milk and sugar boils, and then add the cornstarch mixture by stirring very rapidly to prevent burning or lumping. Continue to stir until mixture thickens. Remove from heat and pour into container to cool, place plastic wrap directly on filling. Chill in refrigerator. If cream filling is made the day before using, beat cream with wire whip to soften and blend for a nicer consistency for filling cream puff shells. Dust with confectionery sugar just before serving.

Note:

By placing plastic wrap directly on filling, it prevents the filling from forming a hard crust. Filling has to be completely cooled before filling shells.

Variations:

I wouldn't change a thing.

PIES

PUMPKIN PIE

This is my mom's recipe. She started baking this pie at least 50 years ago. The combination of spices makes a tasty filling that is creamy in texture.

Ingredients:

1 ¾ cup canned pumpkin
1 tsp. cinnamon
½ tsp. ground ginger
½ tsp. nutmeg
½ tsp. salt

2 eggs beaten
¾ cup sugar
1 ½ cup milk
2 tblp. melted butter

Directions:

Prepare pastry crust for one crust pie. Mix together the pumpkin, spices, salt and sugar. Add beaten eggs and melted butter. Add milk to pumpkin mixture. Pour into 9-inch pie plate lined with unbaked pastry shell.

Preheat Oven: 450 degrees bake pie for 15 minutes. Reduce heat to 350 degrees and bake for about 45 minutes or until crust is well browned. Insert knife in center of pie filling. Filling is done when knife comes out clean.

Note:

Reminder, filling will continue to cook after pie is removed from oven.

CUSTARD PIE

This was one of my dad's favorite pies. My mom created this pie back in the 1940's. It is your basic old fashion custard filling.

Ingredients:

3 cups milk (scalded)
½ cup sugar
Pinch of salt

6 eggs
2 tsp. vanilla

Directions:

Line 9-inch pie plate with pie pastry. Mix slightly beaten eggs with sugar, vanilla and salt. Scald milk. Stir milk gradually into egg mixture. Strain filling mixture into uncooked pie shell.

Preheat Oven: 450 degrees. Bake for 10 minutes. Reduce oven to 325 degrees. Bake 30-35 minutes. Remove pie when knife inserted in center comes out clean.

Note:

To strain filling use fine mesh strainer, this will remove any lumps that occurred when adding milk to eggs.

Variations:

My mom would sprinkle a little nutmeg on the filling before baking.

FRESH STRAWBERRY RHUBARB PIE

Soon after we moved to the country, we started to grow rhubarb and strawberries. After picking our rhubarb and strawberries I would treat my family to this great pie.

Ingredients:

2 cups sugar
2-cup cut-up rhubarb
2 tblp. Butter

⅔ cup flour
3 cup sliced fresh strawberries

Directions:

Mix together sugar and flour. Add rhubarb and strawberries and toss lightly. Pour into a 9-inch pie plates lined with pastry crust; dot with butter. Cover with top crust, which has slits cut in it. Sprinkle with sugar. Bake until crust is nicely browned and juice begins to bubble through slits. Serve slightly warm.

Preheat Oven: 425 degrees
Bake: 40-50 minutes

Note:

Wrap a strip of aluminum foil around edges of pie. This will prevent the pie from burning. Remove foil the last 15 minutes of baking.

Variations:

Instead of full top crust, try putting a lattice pastry on the pie.

FRESH CHERRY PIE

Another way to use the sour cherries that we harvest in summer is this great cherry pie. My husband Tony has this listed as one of his favorite pies. Of course, if there is one pit somewhere in the pie he will be the one to get it.

Ingredients:

2-cup sugar
½ tsp. cinnamon
1 tsp. almond extract

½ cup flour
4 cups fresh sour cherries
2 tblp. Butter

Directions:

Mix together sugar, flour, cinnamon and almond extract. Mix cherries lightly through flour mixture. Pour into a 9-inch pie pan lined with pastry crust; dot with butter. Cover with top crust, which has slits cut in it. Bake until crust is nicely browned and juice begins to bubble through slits.

Preheat Oven: 425 degrees
Bake: 35-45 minutes

Note:

Wrap a strip of aluminum foil around outer edge of pie to prevent burning. Serve slightly warm not hot.

Variations:

I can't think of any way to improve this great pie.

BANANA CREAM PIE

My dad enjoyed desserts. I can't remember how far back this recipe goes. My mom was baking it back in the 1940's.

Ingredients:

3 egg yolks (beaten)   2 cups milk
½ cup sugar   1 tsp. pure vanilla extract
2 tblp. Cornstarch
Sliced bananas to line bottom of cooked pie shell

Directions:

Blend sugar and cornstarch in saucepan. Add beaten eggs to milk and stir into sugar and cornstarch mixture. Cook over medium heat until mixture is thickened. Add vanilla. Pour into 9 inch baked pie shell. Top with meringue (see recipe) bake until meringue is golden brown.

PREHEAT OVEN: 400 degrees
BAKE: 8-10 minutes

Note:

Make sure you seal the meringue to the edge of the pie.

PIE MERINGUE

A great topping for cream and lemon pies. Makes enough for a 9-inch pie.

Ingredients:

3 egg whites
6 tblp. Sugar

¼ tsp. cream of tartar

Directions:

Beat egg whites with cream of tartar until frothy. Gradually beat in sugar, a little at a time. Continue beating until stiff and glossy. Do not under beat. Beat until sugar is dissolved. Pile meringue on hot pie filling, being careful to seal the meringue onto edge of crust to prevent shrinking and weeping. Bake until delicately brown.

PREHEAT OVEN: 400 degrees
BAKE: 8-10 minutes

Note:

It is important that meringue be place on HOT PIE FILLING.

APPLE PIE

In September we start to harvest our apples. We have grown our own apples for the past twenty years. There is nothing like homemade applesauce; except homemade apple pie.

Ingredients:

1-cup sugar
⅓ cup flour
1 ½ tblp. Butter
Pastry for two-crust 9-inch pie (see recipe)

1 tsp. cinnamon
6 to 7 cups sliced apples
1 tblp. Fresh lemon juice

Directions:

Place apples in a large mixing bowl; sprinkle with sugar, cinnamon, flour and lemon juice; mix well. Line pie plate with pastry; fill with apple mixture; dot with butter. Cover with top crust, which has slits cut in it. Seal and flute edges.

PREHEAT OVEN: 425 degrees
BAKE: 50-60 minutes

Note:

Place a narrow stripe of aluminum foil around the edge of the pie. This will prevent the crust from getting to brown. The last 10 minutes remove the foil. Also, Cortland apples work well for this recipe.

Variations:

Sometimes I sprinkle the top of the pie with granulated sugar.

PUDDING

BREAD PUDDING

Growing up in the 1940's and 1950's taught me that nothing was tossed away. Day old bread became bread pudding. My mom could create desserts with a lot of imagination.

Ingredients:

4 eggs
⅔ cup sugar
1-cup milk
12 oz. can evaporated milk
small pieces

1 tsp. vanilla
½ tsp. salt
nutmeg (sprinkle on top)
3 oz. day old bread broken into

Directions:

Beat eggs and sugar together. Scald milk and evaporated milk. Slowly incorporate milk into egg mixture. Add flavoring and salt. Stir bread into egg mixture. Pour into 1 ½ qt. oven proof-baking pan. Dust with nutmeg. Place pan in a water bath, measure water to half waypoint of baking pan.

Preheat Oven: 450 degrees
Lower Oven: 350 degrees

Bake: 20 minutes
Bake: an additional 15-20 minutes

Note:

You may use 1% milk or homogenized milk along with the evaporated milk.

Variations:

In place of nutmeg, try sprinkling cinnamon on top of pudding.

RICE PUDDING

This is an extra special way to serve rice pudding. Using a meringue as a topping creates an elegant dessert.

Ingredients:

4 cup milk
½ cup long grain rice
½ tsp. salt
1 tsp. vanilla
4 egg whites

4 egg yolks
½ cup sugar
2 tblp. Butter
3 tblp. Sugar

Directions:

Bring milk to a boil in a large saucepan. DO NOT BRING TO FOAM STAGE. Stir in rice. Reduce heat to medium-low, cook uncovered, about 18 minutes or until rice is tender. Stir frequently. Combine egg yolks, sugar, butter and vanilla in a medium bowl. Beat until well blended; but not foamy. Stir in 1-cup hot rice mixture into egg mixture. While stirring, pour remaining egg mixture into rice (in saucepan). Bring to a boil stir constantly. Cook one minute or until thick. Pour rice mixture into a greased 2-quart casserole.

Meanwhile, beat egg whites in large bowl on medium speed one minute or until soft peaks form. Gradually add sugar one tablespoon at a time. Beat on high four minutes or until mixture forms stiff, glossy peaks. Immediately spread meringue over rice pudding. Carefully sealing to the edges. Bake, and cool on wire rack. Serve warm or cold.

Preheat Oven: 350 degrees
Bake: 15 minutes
Yield: 8 servings

Note:

Make sure when boiling milk it comes only to a boil. Do not create any foam.

Variations:

You could add ½ cup raisins to rice mixture before pouring into casserole.

SALADS

BROCCOLI SALAD

Sweet and savory salad given to me by my sister-in-law Rita.

Ingredients:
4 cups broccoli florets
½ cup red sweet onion chopped
¼ cup yellow raisins
8 slices bacon crisp fried; broken in pieces

Dressing:
1-cup mayonnaise
¼ cup sugar
2 tblp. Cider vinegar

Directions:
Combine all ingredients and set aside. Mix mayonnaise, sugar and vinegar. Toss salad ingredients with dressing.

Note:
Making this salad the day before serving allows flavors to blend.

Variations:
For a change, use half broccoli and half cauliflower florets. In place of raisins, substitute chopped dates.

WINTER GREEN SALAD

I still haven't figured out why this is called Winter Green Salad. This salad can be served year round. I especially like to serve it when having my card club in for a luncheon.

Ingredients:
SALAD:
¼ cup chopped pecans
8 cups torn assorted greens (iceberg lettuce, spinach, and romaine)
2 cups sliced celery
2 cups green seedless grapes,
Grapes cut in half lengthwise

2 tblp. sugar

1-cup fresh raspberries
3 kiwifruit, peeled and sliced
¼ cup chopped red onion

DRESSING:
¼ cup oil
2 tblp. sugar

2 tblp. White vinegar
½ tsp. salt

Directions:

In small non-stick fry pan, combine pecans and 2 tblp. sugar. Stir over low heat until sugar melts and coats pecans. Remove from heat; spread pecans on waxed paper or foil. Cool; break up any large clumps.

In large bowl, combine greens, celery, grapes, raspberries, kiwi and red onion. In small bowl using wire whisk, blend all dressing ingredients. Pour over salad mixture; add pecans. Toss gently. Serve immediately. Serves: 10 (1-cup) servings.

Note:

It is important that this salad is served as soon as it has been tossed. You want the greens to be crisp when served.

Variations:

In place of seedless green grapes you can substitute seedless red grapes.

AMBROSIA SALAD

This is a very refreshing salad. It goes together fast and can be prepared the day before.

Ingredients:
1 small package instant pistachio pudding
1 (16 oz.) can chunky pineapple   1 (8 oz.) can crushed pineapple
1 cup shredded coconut   1 cup chopped walnuts
16 oz. frozen whipped topping (thawed)
1-cup miniature marshmallows

Directions:
Start by combining the cans of pineapple (including the juice) and sprinkle the pudding over the pineapple and let sit for a couple minutes. Gently mix in the coconut and nuts and then blend in the whipped topping and marshmallows. Place in refrigerator for at least two hours to let the flavors blend together, and then it's ready to serve.

Note:
It is important that you mix this salad with a gent touch. Do not over mix. You could also serve this as a dessert.

Variations:
You can substitute pecans for the chopped walnuts.

PASTA FRUIT SALAD

Acini-di-pepe is pasta. This salad is refreshing and it makes enough to serve a large crowd.

Ingredients:

1-cup acini-di-pepe pasta
1 large can crushed pineapple
4 cups mini marshmallows
8 oz. container whipped topping, thawed

2 small cans mandarin oranges
1 cup white sugar
2 tblp. flour

Directions:

Cook pasta in 3 cups boiling water. Drain oranges and pineapple; reserve juices. In medium size saucepan, combine sugar and flour; stir to blend, add juice from fruits. Cook over medium heat, until thickened stir constantly. Drain pasta when done. In large bowl, combine pasta, fruits and cooked sauce. Place in refrigerator and let set at least 24 hours. Just before serving, add thawed whipped topping mixing thoroughly.

Note:

This is a great salad when you entertaining a large crowd.

Variations:

Try adding a cup chopped walnuts to salad before adding whipped topping.

STRAWBERRY-PRETZEL SQUARES

I have served this as a dessert because it is so elegant. My son Tony started making this when he was a high school student. We have enjoyed serving it at many picnics and during the holidays.

Ingredients:

2 cups finely crushed pretzels
⅔ cup butter melted
¼ cup sugar
1 cup thawed whipped topping
1 pkg. (8 serving size) strawberry Jell-o
1 ½ cups cold water

⅓ cup sugar
12 ounces cream cheese soften
2 tblp. milk
2 cups boiling water

2 pints strawberries, sliced

Directions:

Mix crushed pretzels, ⅓ cup sugar and melted butter. Press firmly into bottom of 13 x 9 inch baking pan. Bake 10 minutes. Cool.

Beat cream cheese, ¼ cup sugar and milk until smooth. Stir in whipped topping. Spread over cooled crust. Refrigerate. Stir boiling water into Jell-o in a large bowl 2 minutes or until completely dissolved. Stir in cold water. Refrigerate 1 ½ hours or until thickened. Stir in strawberries; spoon over cream cheese layer.

Refrigerate 3 hours or until firm. Cut into squares. Garnish with additional whipped topping if you desire.

PREHEAT OVEN: 350 degrees
BAKE: 10 minutes

ANTIPASTO

After trying many combinations of ingredients, this is my family's favorite.

Ingredients:
2 jars marinated artichoke hearts, with liquid (cut artichoke hearts in half)
2 cans black pitted olives (drained)
2 cans pitted large green olives (drained)
2 jars roasted peppers cut into strips
½ lb. sharp Italian cheese cut into 1 inch squares
2 cans chick peas (drained)
1 jar marinated mushrooms, with liquid
1 jar pepperoncini (drained)
¼ lb. Italian hot ham cut into thin strips
¼ cup Italian salad dressing

Directions:
Toss all ingredients together in large bowl. Refrigerate for a couple of hours. Serve over romaine lettuce leafs.

Note:
Do not add cut lettuce to antipasto, it will not keep crisp.

Variations:
There are so many variations to this salad. Whatever you like will work.

SALAD DRESSING

FRENCH SALAD DRESSING

You will say good-bye to bottled dressing after you use this on your salad. A quick dressing to put together because these are ingredients you have in your pantry.

Ingredients:

1 10.5 oz. can tomato soup
1 ½ cup oil (not olive oil)
1 tsp. dry mustard
¼ cup chopped onion (optional)

¾ cup granulated sugar
2 tsp. salt
⅔ cup vinegar

Directions:

You will need a large jar with a screw on top. Place all ingredients in jar and shake well. Makes 1 quart.

Note:

The longer this dressing sets the better the flavor. I suggest you prepare the dressing at least two to three days before you plan to use it.

POPPY SEED SALAD DRESSING

This is a great dressing for your favorite salad greens.

Ingredients:

½ cup honey
3 tblp. White vinegar
1-cup salad oil
1 ½ tblp. finely chopped red onion

½ tsp. salt
½ tbl. Mustard
2 tblp. Olive oil
3 tblp. Poppy seeds

Directions:

Combine all ingredients, except poppy seeds, in large mixing bowl. Mix with a wire whisk. Add poppy seeds and mix well. Pour over your favorite salad greens.

Note:

I suggest salad greens consisting of romaine and spinach leafs.

Variations:

Toss coarse chopped walnuts and orange sections to your salad before serving.

SWEET AND SOUR SALAD DRESSING

This dressing is perfect for a fresh spinach salad. The former pastor of our church shared this recipe at one of his marvelous dinner parties. Thank you Rev. Walt for another great recipe.

Ingredients:

⅓ cup sugar
1 tsp. grated onion
¼ cup cider vinegar
1 tsp. whole celery seeds

1 tsp. salt
1 tsp. dry mustard
¼ cup salad oil (not olive oil)

Directions:

Mix all ingredients in a blender before pouring over salad greens. Toss gently. Garnish salad with fresh sliced mushrooms, orange slices, thin sliced red onion and croutons.

Note:

Remember to use only a vegetable oil.

Variations:

You could use romaine, or iceberg lettuce for this salad. But I personally would stay with fresh spinach.

SOUPS

PASTA FAGIOLO SOUP

This is great soup and a favorite in many Italian families. Especially when you serve it with crusty Italian bread.

Ingredients:

3 tblp. Extra virgin olive oil
1 small onion chopped
1-can cannelini beans, undrained
3 cups escarole rinsed and chopped
1 28 oz. can crush tomatoes

3 carrots chopped
3 cloves garlic, chopped
1 cup ditalini soup pasta
1 49 oz. can chicken broth

Directions:

Heat oil in a 6-quart soup pot on LOW. Add carrots, onion and garlic; cover and cook 4 minutes. Add undrained beans and tomatoes; bring to a simmer and cook 4 minutes. Add escarole, broth and pasta. Season with fresh ground black pepper, salt to taste. Simmer about 8-10 minutes, until pasta is tender. Sprinkle soup with Parmesan or Romano grated cheese. Serve with crusty Italian bread. Serves: 4-6.

Note:

Do not over cook pasta. Make this soup the day before you plan on serving it. The longer this soup sets the better the flavor.

Variations:

Substitute faralline or elbow pasta for ditalini.

POTATO CORN CHOWDER

I have made this soup for many years. It is a hearty and creamy soup.

Ingredients:

6 medium potatoes, peeled and sliced
4 celery stalks, diced
1 quart chicken broth
6 tblp. butter
1 tsp. salt
½ tsp. pepper
⅔ cup canned corn

2 carrots, diced
1 quart water
1 onion, chopped
6 tblp. All-purpose flour
¼ tsp. dill
1 ½ cup milk

Directions:

In a large saucepan, cook potatoes, carrots and celery with water and chicken broth until tender, about 20 minutes. Drain, reserving liquid and setting vegetables aside. In the same saucepan, sauté onion in butter until soft. Stir in flour, dill, salt and pepper; gradually add milk, stirring constantly until thickened. Gently stir in cooked vegetables and corn. Add 1 cup or more of reserved cooking liquid until soup is at desired consistency.

Yield: 8-10 servings (about 2 ½ quarts)

Note:

Use medium low heat when adding milk to flour mixture. Bring mixture to a slow simmer.

Variations:

If you are not fond of dill, eliminate it from the recipe.

CREAMY TOMATO BASIL SOUP

Since we grow our own tomatoes and sweet basil, this soup finds its way to our table every fall.

Ingredients:

⅓ cup vegetable oil
1 tsp. minced garlic
2 (14 ½ oz.) cans chicken broth
¼ cup chopped fresh basil
½ tsp. salt
1 ½ lbs. Tomatoes, peeled, seeded and chopped

1 medium onion, chopped
¼ cup flour
½ cup half and half
1 tsp. sugar
¼ tsp. pepper

Directions:

In large saucepan heat oil; over medium-low heat sauté onion and garlic until tender. <u>Do not brown.</u> Stir in flour; cook one minute. Add remaining ingredients. Stir until well blended. Bring to a boil; reduce heat and simmer, uncovered, 20 minutes. Pour small batches into blender or food processor, puree until smooth.

Yield: 6 servings

CHUNKY VEGETARIAN CHILI

This chili is high in fiber and low in fat. I suggest you make it a day or two before you plan on serving it. The longer it sets the better it tastes.

Ingredients:

1 large onion diced
1 ½ cups matchstick carrots
2-15 oz. cans dark kidney beans
1-28 oz. can Italian crushed tomatoes with herbs
1-28 oz. can crush pineapple drained
2 tblp. Chili powder
1 clove garlic chopped

1 green pepper chopped
1-8 oz. package sliced mushrooms

Directions:

Combine all ingredients in 6-quart saucepan. Mix well. Cook on medium heat. Reduce to a simmer and cook for 1½ hour.

Note:

Stir occasionally to prevent sticking.

Variations:

Use red bell pepper in place of green.

BEANS AND GREENS

When you are looking for comfort food, try this soup. I experimented with many ingredients until I found this combination worked.

Ingredients:
2 tblp extra virgin olive oil
4 medium carrots chopped
2 cloves garlic minced
2 cups water
1-large head escarole washed and chopped
15 oz. can cannelini beans with Juice

2 medium onions chopped
1-large can chicken broth
Salt and pepper to taste

Directions:
Place olive oil in large saucepan over medium-high heat; add carrots, onion and garlic, sauté 3 minutes; season with salt and pepper. Add beans, chicken broth and water. Bring to a simmer. Return to a boil; add escarole. Simmer for 45 minutes. Ladle into soup bowl and garnish with 1 tblp. Parmesan cheese. Serve with Italian rolls.

Note:
Instead of adding the complete can of cannelini beans, measure 1 cup and crush with a fork; return to saucepan. This will give you thicker soup.

Variations:
In place of the escarole, use rabbi. You will have to clean rabbi. Cut into thirds, cook in salted water before adding to soup mixture.

GREEN SPLIT PEA AND HAM SOUP

When fall arrives it's time to get ready for homemade soup. I enjoy cooking for my husband Tony. Split pea soup with ham is one of his favorites.

Ingredients:

1 lb. dry green split peas
2 packets chicken bouillon
¼ lb. smoked ham, diced
1 medium onion, diced
Salt and pepper to taste

1 clove garlic, minced
1 medium carrot, diced
1 stalk celery, diced
6 cups water

Directions:

Sort and rinse peas. In a 6 to 8 quart saucepan, combine all ingredients; bring to a boil. Reduce heat, cover and simmer until peas are tender. Add more water if necessary. Top each serving with croutons, if desired. Serves 6.

Note:

This soup tends to get very thick after it cools. If it is too thick for you, just add some canned chicken broth.

Variations:

When you bake a ham with shank bone, use the bone, leaving some ham in tacked, in place of the smoke ham. In place of the dry green split peas, you may use the dry yellow split peas. If you prefer this soup be only vegetarian, just leave out the smoked ham. In order to still have the ham flavor, use a few drops of liquid smoke.

VEGETABLES

THREE-BEAN BAKED BEANS

This handwritten recipe was tucked away in my recipe box. I wish I could remember who gave it to me. Don't get discouraged by how many ingredients you need. It goes together easily and does not compare to the old fashion baked bean dish, great for picnics and special occasions.

Ingredients:

½ pound ground beef
½ cup chopped onion
⅓ cup packed brown sugar
¼ cup ketchup
2 tblp. molasses
2 (16 oz.) cans pork & beans undrained
1 (16 oz) can butter beans, rinsed and drained
1 (16 oz) can kidney beans, rinsed and drained

5 bacon strips, diced
½ tsp. salt
¼ cup sugar
¼ cup barbecue sauce
2 tblp. Prepared mustard
½ tsp. chili powder

Directions:

In large skillet or saucepan over medium heat, brown beef, bacon and onion; drain. Add beans. Combine remaining ingredients; stir into bean mixture. Pour into a greased 2-½ quart baking dish. Baked uncovered.

Preheat Oven: 350 degrees
Bake: 1 hour or until beans reach desired thickness
YIELD: 12 SERVINGS

Note:

Beans will seem loose in texture continue baking until they thicken.

Variations:

Substitute ground turkey for the ground beef.

SWEET-AND-SOUR RED CABBAGE

In 1958 my husband Tony was stationed in Germany with the United State Army. I was able to join him and resided in Germany for eighteen months. It was a wonderful experience. We lived with a German family. Our landlady shared her favorite red cabbage dish with me.

Ingredients:

¼ cup raisins   ¼ cup sugar
¼ cup vinegar (apple cider)   ½ tsp. salt
⅛ tsp.pepper   1 tblp. margarine or butter
1 medium head red cabbage, shredded (6cups)
1 medium apple, peeled and finely chopped

Directions:

In a large skillet cook cabbage, apple, and raisins, covered, in a small amount of boiling water for 5-7 minutes or until crisp-tender; drain. In a small mixing bowl combine sugar, vinegar, salt and pepper; stir until sugar is dissolved. Add to cabbage mixture in skillet. Add margarine or butter. Cook, covered, for 3 to 4 minutes or until heated through, stirring twice. Makes 6 to 8 servings.

Note:

This was usually served with pork or sauerbraten. You have to like cabbage to enjoy this dish.

Variations:

I have always followed the recipe just as it was written.

TWICE-BAKED POTATOES

These potatoes can be assembled up to 24 hours ahead of time. Cover and refrigerate. When you're ready to bake, remove them from the refrigerator while you are preheating the oven.

Ingredients:

6 large russet potatoes
¾ to 1 cup half-and-half cream
3 tblp. finely chopped onion
½ tsp. salt
6 oz. shredded cheddar cheese

½ cup butter softened
3 tblp. crumbled cooked bacon
1 tblp. snipped chives
Dash pepper
Paprika

Directions:

Bake potatoes at 375 degrees for 1 hour or until soft. Allow to cool. Cut a thin slice off the top of each potato. Scoop out the pulp and place in a bowl; add butter and mash the pulp. Blend in half-and-half, bacon, onion, chives, salt, and pepper and 1 cup of cheese. Spoon into potato shells. Top with remaining cheese and sprinkle with paprika. Place on a baking sheet.

Bake, uncovered, at 375 degrees for 25-30 minutes; until heated through.

Note:

Line baking sheet with parchment paper; easy clean up if cheese melts on pan.

Variations:

Milk can be substituted for the half-and-half and margarine can be used in place of the butter.

EGGPLANT PARMESAN (NO FRYING)

To make this dish the traditional way, you need to fry the eggplant before baking. I have eliminated that step by baking the breaded eggplant before adding the sauce for final preparation.

Ingredients:
1 medium eggplant peeled
2 cups seasoned Italian breadcrumbs
¼ cup grated Parmesan cheese
1 tsp. garlic powder
Salt and pepper to taste
3 eggs beaten
1 jar spaghetti sauce

Directions:
Combine breadcrumbs, garlic powder, grated cheese, salt and pepper; set aside. Peel eggplant, cut into ¼ inch slices. Dip eggplant in breadcrumbs, into beaten eggs, back into breadcrumbs. Set aside. On a cookie sheet lined with aluminum foil, place breaded eggplant slices in a single layer. Spray eggplant with Pam bake for 15 minutes on each side.

In a 13 x 9 inch baking pan, cover bottom of pan with sauce, place one layer of eggplant in pan, cover with sauce, and sprinkle with grated Parmesan cheese. Continue the layering process until all eggplant is used. Cover with foil return to oven, bake for 45 minutes.

PREHEAT OVEN: 350 degrees
BAKE: According to directions in recipe

Note:
Using commercial spaghetti sauce works great. Homemade sauce can also be used.

Variations:
During the last 10 minutes of baking you could sprinkle shredded mozzarella cheese on top of the eggplant. Leave foil off while cheese melts.

ESCAROLE WITH BREADCRUMBS

I have used escarole in soup, in salads, and mixed with pasta; but this combination is one of my favorites.

Ingredients:

1 large head escarole
¼ cup grated Parmesan cheese
1 tsp. garlic powder
3 tblp. Extra virgin olive oil

1-cup Italian style breadcrumbs
Salt and pepper to taste
1 clove garlic minced
¼ cup water

Directions:

Separate escarole, wash, cut leafs in half. Place escarole in salted boiling water; cook 2-3 minutes; drain in colander. Combine breadcrumbs, Parmesan cheese, salt, and pepper and garlic powder, set aside. Place escarole in mixing bowl, add minced garlic; olive oil, mix well. Arrange escarole in ovenproof baking pan; cover with breadcrumbs mixture, sprinkle with water. Cover and bake.

PREHEAT OVEN: 350 degrees
BAKE: 25-30 minutes

Note:

You can save the inside of the escarole, the white tender leafs and use them in a salad. Reminder, these will have a slight bitter taste compared to regular leaf lettuce.

Variations:

This combination works for me.

ABOUT THE AUTHOR

Having roots in Italy and Canada, and being a third generation Italian, Annette enjoys cooking for Family and Friends. She was born and raised in Canandaigua, New York; nestled at the north end of one of the New York Finger Lakes, located south of Rochester, New York.

In her spare time, Annette enjoys traveling with her husband Tony, gardening, singing in her church choir; is a Eucharistic minister at her church; enjoys spending time with her five granddaughters, and two grandsons. She also looks forward to the time she spends with friends' in her card club.

Living in a Small Town has many rewards for Annette. It has allowed her to spend quality time with Family and Friends that have been a special part of her life.

Annette has written The Small Town Big Kitchen Cookbook as the follow up cookbook to her son Anthony's cookbook, The Big City Small Kitchen Cookbook.

0-595-29161-9